The Texts Of The Sumerians

Introduction

The ancient civilization of **Sumer**, which flourished in southern Mesopotamia (modern-day Iraq) around 4500 to 1900 BCE, is widely regarded as the cradle of civilization. Sumerians were among the first to develop cities, writing systems, complex social structures, and monumental architecture. Their contributions laid the foundation for much of what we understand as modern society, from law and governance to literature, religion, and art.

At the heart of Sumerian society was their profound belief in the divine. The Sumerians viewed their gods not only as powerful supernatural beings but also as direct influences on every aspect of life—natural, political, and personal. The writings they left behind, especially in the form of **hymns**, **prayers**, **inscriptions**, and **legal texts**, reflect this deeply intertwined relationship between the divine and the mortal world. These texts, often inscribed on clay tablets and monuments, were not only religious expressions but also vital tools for political power, economic stability, and social order.

This book brings together a collection of **Sumerian writings**, showcasing the diversity and depth of their literary and religious traditions. From the **hymns of Enheduanna**, the first known author in human history, to the **Sumerian King List** and the **Code of Ur-Nammu**, these texts offer insights into a world where gods, kings, and common people lived in intricate connection. The texts included here span the realms of law, morality, ritual, and personal devotion, reflecting the complexity of Sumerian thought and their advanced social structure.

Enheduanna's hymns, particularly those dedicated to the goddess Inanna, reveal the emotional and spiritual life of a priestess whose authority extended beyond the temple and into the political sphere. As a high priestess and daughter of the Akkadian king Sargon, Enheduanna's works were both devotional and propagandistic, helping to unify the Sumerian and Akkadian empires under a shared religious framework.

The **Instructions of Shuruppak**, an early wisdom text, provides advice on living a moral and responsible life. The proverbs and teachings offer practical guidance on everything from family relations to ethical conduct and the proper treatment of others. These early teachings laid the groundwork for later ethical and philosophical thought in the region.

The **cylinder seals** and **monumental inscriptions** of Sumerian rulers tell a story of kingship that was divinely sanctioned. Kings such as Ur-Nammu and Hammurabi justified their reigns through their relationship with the gods, often commemorating their achievements in law, warfare, and temple-building on steles and monuments. These texts were not only declarations of power but also tools for ensuring the legacy of their rule across time.

The **Code of Ur-Nammu**, one of the earliest known legal codes, reveals the Sumerians' emphasis on justice and order. Rather than relying solely on retribution, many of the laws focused on fines and compensation, reflecting a society that valued stability and fairness. The legal codes that followed, such as the famous **Code of Hammurabi**, built upon this foundation, further refining the principles of justice and governance.

Together, these writings form a rich tapestry that allows us to glimpse the world of ancient Sumer—a world where divine power, human authority, and moral law were inextricably linked. The texts in this collection provide more than just historical documentation; they offer a window into the minds and hearts of one of humanity's first great civilizations. Through their hymns, legal systems, and wisdom literature, the Sumerians sought to understand their place in the cosmos and establish a lasting order for their society.

By exploring these ancient writings, we can appreciate how deeply these early Mesopotamians influenced the cultures that followed, from the Akkadians and Babylonians to the broader ancient Near East and beyond. Their innovations in writing, law, religion, and governance continue to resonate today, reminding us of the enduring legacy of one of the world's first civilizations.

This book serves as both an introduction to and a celebration of Sumerian culture, preserving the voices of a long-gone era and offering timeless insights into human nature, society, and the divine. Through these ancient texts, we are invited to reflect on the common threads that connect us to the people of Sumer, whose contributions to the development of civilization remain invaluable.

Cuneiform: Thought to be The First Writing System

Cuneiform, developed by the **Sumerians** around 3400–3000 BCE in Mesopotamia, is widely regarded as one of the earliest known writing systems. The word *cuneiform* comes from the Latin word "cuneus," meaning "wedge," and "form," referring to the wedge-shaped marks that made up the script. Initially, it began as a series of pictographs, where simple images represented objects or ideas. Over time, these pictographs became more abstract and were standardized into the wedge-shaped marks that give cuneiform its distinctive appearance.

Evolution of Cuneiform

1. **Early Pictographs**:
    - In its earliest form, cuneiform was a system of pictographs, where symbols directly represented physical objects. For example, a picture of a fish would represent the word for "fish." This early system was mostly used for record-keeping, such as counting livestock or documenting grain storage, especially in a growing agricultural society where tracking resources was crucial.
2. **Phonetic Elements**:
    - As the system evolved, the pictographs began to take on phonetic values. This allowed for the representation of more abstract ideas and the recording of spoken language. The transition from pure pictographs to symbols that represented syllables or sounds marked a significant development in writing systems, as it

enabled the documentation of language itself, not just physical objects or numbers.
3. **Standardization and Use of a Stylus**:
    - Sumerians wrote cuneiform on clay tablets using a reed stylus, which was pressed into the wet clay to form the wedge-shaped marks. The triangular or wedge-shaped tip of the stylus created distinctive impressions that became standardized across the region. The script's shapes could be modified depending on the angle and direction the stylus was pressed, which allowed for the creation of a broad range of characters.
4. **Logographic and Phonetic Elements**:
    - Over time, cuneiform evolved into a **logophonetic** system, meaning it combined logograms (symbols representing words or concepts) and syllabic signs (symbols representing sounds or syllables). This allowed the writing system to record not only names and simple phrases but also complex ideas, making it suitable for a variety of contexts, such as literature, law, administration, and education.

Purposes and Uses of Cuneiform

Cuneiform was used for a wide range of purposes, reflecting the complexity of Sumerian society and its needs. Some of the main uses of cuneiform included:

1. **Economic Transactions and Record Keeping**:
    - One of the primary reasons for the development of cuneiform was to keep track of economic transactions. Early clay tablets were often used to document agricultural

records, taxes, trade agreements, and the distribution of goods. These records were essential for managing the surplus of crops, livestock, and other resources, especially as Sumerian city-states became more urbanized and complex.

2. **Legal Codes and Governance**:
    - Cuneiform was crucial for the codification of laws. The **Code of Ur-Nammu** (circa 2100 BCE), one of the earliest known legal codes, was written in cuneiform. Later, the famous **Code of Hammurabi** (circa 1750 BCE), which included detailed laws and punishments, was also inscribed using this system. The ability to record and enforce laws helped establish centralized governance and created a legal framework for Sumerian and later Babylonian societies.

3. **Literature and Poetry**:
    - Cuneiform was also used to record literature, including some of the earliest known stories and myths. The most famous example of Sumerian literature written in cuneiform is the **Epic of Gilgamesh**, which dates back to around 2100 BCE. This epic, one of the world's oldest surviving literary works, tells the story of Gilgamesh, a legendary king of Uruk, and explores themes of friendship, heroism, and the quest for immortality.

4. **Religious Texts and Hymns**:
    - Cuneiform was used to inscribe hymns, prayers, and religious texts on clay tablets and temple walls. Many of these texts were dedicated to Sumerian deities, and they were central to the religious and ceremonial life

of Sumer. In fact, temples were often the administrative centers where many records, including religious ones, were kept.
5. **Education and Administration**:
    - Schools for scribes, known as **edubbas** ("tablet houses"), were established in Sumerian society. These schools trained young men to become scribes, a highly respected and essential profession, as cuneiform was complex and difficult to master. Scribes were responsible for maintaining the bureaucratic machinery of the state, including writing official correspondence, managing archives, and documenting legal and commercial matters.
6. **Diplomacy and International Relations**:
    - Cuneiform was also used as a diplomatic language across the ancient Near East. The **Amarna Letters**, a collection of diplomatic correspondence between Egypt and other powerful states of the time, were written in cuneiform. These letters document alliances, treaties, and trade agreements, showcasing the influence of the writing system beyond Sumer and into other regions like Egypt, the Hittite Empire, and Assyria.

Widespread Influence and Legacy of Cuneiform

Cuneiform was not limited to the Sumerians. Over time, the writing system was adapted by various other cultures and empires in Mesopotamia, including the **Akkadians**, **Babylonians**, and **Assyrians**. Each of these cultures made their own modifications to the script, but the core principles remained the same. As a result, cuneiform became a unifying script for the region, even as different languages were spoken.

Cuneiform was in use for over 3,000 years, from the rise of Sumer in the fourth millennium BCE until its eventual decline around the first century CE. It was one of the longest-used writing systems in history.

Decipherment of Cuneiform

For many centuries, cuneiform remained undeciphered. The script was first rediscovered in the 19th century during excavations of ancient Mesopotamian sites, including **Nineveh** and **Babylon**. Scholars worked for decades to understand the writing system, and one of the key breakthroughs came from the study of the **Behistun Inscription**, a multilingual inscription carved into a cliff in what is now Iran. This inscription, commissioned by the Persian king **Darius the Great**, was written in Old Persian, Elamite, and Babylonian, providing the linguistic "Rosetta Stone" that helped scholars finally unlock the meaning of cuneiform.

British archaeologist **Henry Rawlinson** played a crucial role in deciphering the script in the 19th century. By comparing the cuneiform signs in the three languages, scholars were able to gradually work out the meanings of the symbols, leading to a fuller understanding of the languages and cultures of ancient Mesopotamia.

Significance of Cuneiform

Cuneiform was revolutionary because it marked the beginning of recorded history. Before the advent of writing, knowledge, stories, and traditions were passed down orally. With cuneiform, for the first time in human history, ideas, laws, religious beliefs, and personal transactions could be preserved in a tangible form. The creation of written records allowed for the development of complex legal systems, bureaucracies, and literature, fundamentally changing how societies were organized.

The legacy of cuneiform extends far beyond Mesopotamia. By documenting everything from the mundane (such as grain accounts) to the profound (such as the first known literature and law codes), cuneiform set the stage for the development of writing systems that followed. It represents a monumental step in human history, bridging the gap between prehistory and recorded civilization.

Conclusion

Cuneiform is a cornerstone of ancient history and human civilization. It was not just a method for recording information; it was a tool that allowed societies to grow more complex, to preserve knowledge, and to communicate across time and space. From economic transactions and administrative records to epic poetry and diplomatic correspondence, cuneiform had a profound impact on the development of early societies and remains one of the most important legacies of the ancient world.

The Sumerians were one of the earliest known civilizations, originating in the region of southern Mesopotamia (modern-day Iraq) around 4500 to 1900 BCE. They are credited with developing many foundational aspects of human culture, particularly in the fields of writing, governance, religion, and architecture.

Key Aspects of Sumerian Civilization:

1. **Writing System – Cuneiform**:
   The Sumerians are credited with developing one of the earliest known writing systems, called *cuneiform*. This system began as pictographs and evolved into wedge-shaped marks on clay tablets. Cuneiform was used for various purposes, including recording economic transactions, laws, and literature, such as the famous *Epic of Gilgamesh*, one of the world's oldest literary works.
2. **City-States**:
   Sumer was not a unified empire but a collection of independent city-states, such as Ur, Uruk, and Lagash. Each city-state had its own ruler and patron deity. The Sumerians built large cities with advanced infrastructure, including temples (ziggurats), palaces, and irrigation systems for agriculture.
3. **Ziggurats**:
   One of the most notable architectural contributions from the Sumerians were the ziggurats—massive terraced structures that served as religious temples. The ziggurat of Ur is one of the best-preserved examples. These temples were dedicated to the gods, with the belief that the gods descended to the top of the ziggurats.
4. **Religion**:
   Sumerian religion was polytheistic, meaning they worshipped multiple gods and goddesses, each representing natural forces or aspects of life. Their deities included Anu (the sky god), Enlil (god of air and storms), and Inanna (goddess of love and war).

Religion was deeply intertwined with politics, and the rulers were often seen as intermediaries between the gods and the people.

5. **Government and Law**:
Sumerian city-states were governed by kings, often referred to as *lugals*. The concept of kingship was divine, and the rulers were thought to have a close relationship with the gods. The Sumerians also developed early systems of law, with the *Code of Ur-Nammu* being one of the earliest surviving legal codes.

6. **Agriculture and Economy**:
Sumerian society was heavily dependent on agriculture, especially the cultivation of barley and wheat. They developed sophisticated irrigation systems to control the flooding of the Tigris and Euphrates rivers. Trade was also vital, with the Sumerians trading surplus crops, wool, and textiles for metals, timber, and precious stones from neighboring regions.

7. **Technological and Mathematical Achievements**:
The Sumerians made significant advancements in mathematics and technology. They developed the sexagesimal (base 60) system, which is still used today in the measurement of time (60 seconds, 60 minutes). They also invented the wheel, which was used for pottery making and later for transportation.

8. **Decline**:
The Sumerian civilization eventually declined due to various factors, including environmental degradation, overuse of agricultural land, and external invasions by neighboring peoples like the Akkadians and Amorites. The Akkadian Empire, under Sargon the Great, absorbed many aspects of Sumerian culture and spread them throughout Mesopotamia.

The legacy of the Sumerians had a profound impact on subsequent civilizations in the region, particularly the Babylonians and Assyrians, and their innovations in writing, law, and governance laid the foundations for many aspects of modern society.

The belief in and understanding of Sumerian civilization comes largely from the discovery of their written records, primarily in the form of *cuneiform tablets*. These texts cover a wide range of subjects, from administrative records and legal codes to religious hymns, literature, and inscriptions on monuments. Some key writings and artifacts that have illuminated the Sumerian world include:

1. The Epic of Gilgamesh

- **What it tells us**: The *Epic of Gilgamesh* is one of the oldest surviving works of literature and provides insights into Sumerian mythology, religion, and views on kingship. It tells the story of King Gilgamesh of Uruk, his quest for immortality, and his friendship with the wild man Enkidu. This epic reveals the Sumerians' views on gods, human mortality, and heroism.
- **Importance**: This text highlights Sumerian values and belief systems, showing their ideas about fate, the afterlife, and the relationship between humans and gods. It also gives us historical insights into their rulers and city-states.

2. The Code of Ur-Nammu

- **What it tells us**: The *Code of Ur-Nammu* is one of the oldest known law codes, dating back to the 21st century BCE. It provides laws covering theft, assault, slavery, marriage, and property rights.

Penalties often included fines rather than the harsher "eye for an eye" punishments found in later codes, like Hammurabi's.
- **Importance**: This code gives us a glimpse into Sumerian legal structures, social norms, and the authority of kings. It shows how justice was administered and what values the society held regarding property, personal rights, and the roles of different classes.

3. The Sumerian King List

- **What it tells us**: This ancient manuscript lists the names of Sumerian kings, the lengths of their reigns, and some significant events during their rule. It begins with mythical kings who supposedly reigned for thousands of years and transitions to historical rulers, giving a sense of both myth and fact in Sumerian political history.
- **Importance**: The *Sumerian King List* provides a semi-historical record of the succession of kings and the rise and fall of different city-states. While some kings on the list are legendary, others can be cross-referenced with archaeological evidence, helping historians establish timelines for early Mesopotamian history.

4. Temple Hymns and Religious Texts

- **What they tell us**: The Sumerians composed hymns to their gods, many of which were found on clay tablets. These hymns were used in religious ceremonies and offer insights into Sumerian deities, the roles of temples, and the relationship between humans and gods.

- **Importance**: These texts reveal the Sumerians' religious practices and their devotion to various gods. They also highlight the importance of the temple in Sumerian society, not only as a religious center but also as an economic and administrative hub.

5. Administrative and Economic Tablets

- **What they tell us**: Tens of thousands of cuneiform tablets from Sumer have been discovered, detailing economic transactions, tax records, contracts, and inventories of goods. These were often found in temple archives and provide evidence of a highly organized and bureaucratic society.
- **Importance**: These documents give us a clear view of how the Sumerian economy functioned, the management of agricultural resources, and the importance of trade. They also reveal the central role of temples in administering land, labor, and resources.

6. Inscriptions on Monuments and Steles

- **What they tell us**: Inscriptions on monuments, such as the Stele of the Vultures, commemorate military victories and other significant events. The Stele of the Vultures, for example, details the victory of King Eannatum of Lagash over the neighboring city of Umma.
- **Importance**: These inscriptions provide valuable historical details about wars, political rivalries, and alliances between city-states. They also serve as evidence of the Sumerians' sense of historical documentation and commemoration of achievements.

7. The Instructions of Shuruppak

- **What it tells us**: This wisdom text is a collection of moral and ethical guidelines supposedly written by a father, Shuruppak, to his son. It contains advice on how to live a good life, treat others fairly, and succeed in a competitive world.
- **Importance**: The *Instructions of Shuruppak* is an early example of didactic literature, providing insights into Sumerian values, social norms, and family dynamics. It also shows a concern for wisdom and education in Sumerian society.

8. Cylinder Seals

- **What they tell us**: Cylinder seals were small, engraved stones that were rolled over wet clay to leave an impression. These seals were used to mark property or documents and often depicted scenes of gods, daily life, or mythological figures.
- **Importance**: While not purely written texts, cylinder seals offer valuable visual evidence of Sumerian religion, art, and the interactions between humans and gods. They also provide insights into the administrative practices of Sumerian society, as they were often used to authenticate records.

9. Enheduanna's Hymns

- **What they tell us**: Enheduanna, the daughter of Sargon of Akkad, was a high priestess and one of the earliest known authors. Her hymns to the goddess Inanna reveal a deep connection between

the rulers and the divine, and they express personal devotion as well as political propaganda.
- **Importance**: These hymns are significant as they are among the first literary works attributed to a known individual, marking the beginning of authorial identity. They also reveal the role of women, especially high priestesses, in Sumerian religious life.

Conclusion:

The vast array of written records from Sumer gives us a detailed picture of Sumerian civilization—its government, religion, social structures, and daily life. Cuneiform tablets, religious hymns, legal codes, and literary works like *The Epic of Gilgamesh* are among the most important sources that help us understand the contributions and history of the Sumerians. These texts demonstrate the sophistication of Sumerian society and their influence on later civilizations in Mesopotamia and beyond.

The Epic of Gilgamesh

is one of the oldest known literary works, originating from ancient Mesopotamia and written in Akkadian using cuneiform script. Its complete version comes from tablets discovered in the ruins of the Library of Ashurbanipal at Nineveh, although earlier Sumerian versions of parts of the story have been found. The epic is a composite work formed from several versions and translations across time, and many scholars have reconstructed it from various sources.

Below is a high-level summary of the complete text, divided into its twelve tablets:

Tablet I: The Coming of Enkidu

- The story begins with an introduction to **Gilgamesh**, the king of **Uruk**. He is a powerful but tyrannical leader, exploiting his people and forcing them into labor. The gods hear the people's complaints and create **Enkidu**, a wild man who lives with animals, to challenge Gilgamesh's strength.
- **Enkidu** is eventually tamed by a temple prostitute named Shamhat, who teaches him human ways. Enkidu learns of Gilgamesh's tyranny and sets out to confront him.

Tablet II: Enkidu and Gilgamesh Become Friends

- Enkidu arrives in Uruk and challenges Gilgamesh. They engage in a fierce wrestling match, but

- Gilgamesh wins. Despite their rivalry, the two become close friends and allies.
- Gilgamesh proposes that they go on an adventure to the **Cedar Forest** to kill the guardian monster **Humbaba**.

Tablet III: Preparation for the Journey

- The elders of Uruk warn Gilgamesh of the dangers of the journey, but Gilgamesh ignores their advice. He and Enkidu prepare for their expedition, making offerings to the gods, particularly **Shamash**, the sun god, asking for protection.

Tablet IV: The Journey to the Cedar Forest

- Gilgamesh and Enkidu travel to the Cedar Forest. Along the way, Gilgamesh has ominous dreams, which Enkidu interprets positively, encouraging his friend to continue. They arrive at the Cedar Forest, ready for battle.

Tablet V: The Battle with Humbaba

- Gilgamesh and Enkidu face **Humbaba**, the monstrous guardian of the Cedar Forest. After a fierce battle, they defeat Humbaba, despite his pleas for mercy.
- They cut down the sacred cedar trees and make a raft to return to Uruk with the wood. They also honor the gods with their victory.

Tablet VI: Ishtar and the Bull of Heaven

- Back in Uruk, the goddess **Ishtar** falls in love with Gilgamesh and proposes marriage, but he rejects her, insulting her past lovers.
- In retaliation, Ishtar sends the **Bull of Heaven** to punish Gilgamesh and Enkidu. Together, they kill the Bull, which angers the gods further.

Tablet VII: The Death of Enkidu

- The gods decree that one of the heroes must be punished for the killing of the Bull of Heaven, and they choose Enkidu. He falls ill and begins to waste away.
- Enkidu curses his fate, expressing sorrow for abandoning his wild, free life and condemning Shamhat for civilizing him. However, before his death, he reconciles with his fate.

Tablet VIII: The Mourning of Gilgamesh

- Gilgamesh is devastated by Enkidu's death and mourns deeply. He orders a grand funeral for his friend, constructing a magnificent statue in his honor. Gilgamesh is haunted by the inevitability of death and begins to fear his own mortality.

Tablet IX: The Quest for Immortality

- Stricken by the fear of death, Gilgamesh embarks on a journey to find **Utnapishtim**, a man who was granted immortality by the gods after surviving a great flood.

- Gilgamesh travels through dangerous landscapes, including the **Twin Peaks** and the **Garden of the Gods**, eventually crossing the Waters of Death to reach Utnapishtim.

Tablet X: Gilgamesh Meets Utnapishtim

- Gilgamesh meets **Siduri**, a tavern-keeper, who advises him to abandon his quest and enjoy life. However, Gilgamesh persists and finally meets Utnapishtim.
- Utnapishtim tells Gilgamesh that immortality is not meant for mortals, recounting the story of the flood and how he was granted eternal life by the gods.

Tablet XI: The Story of the Flood and Gilgamesh's Return

- Utnapishtim recounts how the gods decided to send a flood to wipe out humanity. He was instructed by the god **Ea** to build a boat and save his family and animals. After the flood, the gods regretted their decision, and Utnapishtim and his wife were granted immortality.
- Utnapishtim challenges Gilgamesh to stay awake for six days and seven nights to prove his worthiness for immortality, but Gilgamesh fails the test.
- However, Utnapishtim's wife convinces him to tell Gilgamesh about a plant at the bottom of the sea that can restore youth. Gilgamesh retrieves the plant but loses it when a serpent steals it while he bathes.
- Gilgamesh returns to Uruk, accepting that immortality is beyond his reach, and resolves to be a wise and good king.

Tablet XII: Enkidu's Spirit and the Underworld (Appendix)

- This tablet is considered a later addition and does not fit neatly into the rest of the epic. In this section, Gilgamesh has a vision of Enkidu's spirit, who describes the bleak and miserable existence of the dead in the underworld.
- This reinforces the Sumerian concept of the afterlife as a grim place, even for heroes.

Key Themes:

- **Mortality and Immortality**: Gilgamesh's journey is one of self-discovery and acceptance of human mortality.
- **Friendship**: The bond between Gilgamesh and Enkidu is central to the story and drives much of the plot.
- **Heroism**: Gilgamesh seeks to achieve lasting fame through heroic deeds but ultimately learns that wisdom and leadership are more important.
- **The Role of the Gods**: The gods in the epic are capricious, often intervening in human affairs for reasons of personal pride or revenge.

Existing Versions:

The standard Akkadian version of the epic was compiled by the scholar Sin-liqe-unninni around 1200 BCE. The Sumerian poems, on which the epic is based, are older, dating back to around 2100 BCE. The Akkadian version is primarily preserved in a collection of twelve clay tablets from the Library of Ashurbanipal in Nineveh (7th century BCE).

For a more in-depth exploration, many translations and reconstructions exist, but because some tablets are incomplete or fragmented, not all versions are identical.

1. The Epic of Gilgamesh

- **Found**: The earliest fragments of the *Epic of Gilgamesh* were found in the ancient city of Nineveh (modern-day Iraq) during excavations of the Library of Ashurbanipal by British archaeologist Austen Henry Layard in the mid-19th century. However, Sumerian versions of the story have been discovered in other locations, such as Ur and Nippur.
- **Currently housed**:
    - The tablets from Nineveh are housed in the **British Museum**, London.
    - Other fragments from Ur and Nippur are held in museums like the **University of Pennsylvania Museum of Archaeology and Anthropology**, Philadelphia, and the **Iraq Museum**, Baghdad.

Tablet I: The Coming of Enkidu

Introduction to Gilgamesh and Uruk

Gilgamesh, king of Uruk, was two-thirds god and one-third man, with unparalleled strength and wisdom. His city, Uruk, was known for its great walls and its temples dedicated to the gods Anu (the sky god) and Ishtar (the goddess of love and war).

Lines 1–8 He who saw everything, Gilgamesh, who knew all things, explored all things, he was wise and learned the ways of the world. He discovered hidden secrets and brought back stories of times before the flood. He journeyed far and wide and became weary but earned his fame. He had engraved his story on stone tablets for future generations to learn.

Lines 9–20 Gilgamesh was the mighty king of the city of Uruk. He built the strong walls of the city and the temples of the gods. The people of Uruk loved their city but feared their king. Gilgamesh, in his arrogance, oppressed the people of Uruk. He took young men for his army and forced the young women to serve him.

The Creation of Enkidu

Lines 21–32 The people of Uruk cried out to the gods to stop Gilgamesh. The gods heard their plea, and the goddess Aruru, the creator of mankind, fashioned a rival for Gilgamesh, a wild man named **Enkidu**, from clay. Enkidu was covered in hair, lived in the wild, and ran with the animals. He knew nothing of human life or civilization.

Lines 33–60 Enkidu lived among the gazelles, drank with the animals at the waterholes, and freed them from the traps set by hunters. One day, a trapper saw Enkidu and was terrified by the sight of this wild man. The trapper's livelihood was threatened because Enkidu was freeing all the animals from his traps.

Lines 61–78 The trapper told his father about this wild man and asked for advice. His father told him to go to Uruk and speak to Gilgamesh. The trapper was instructed to ask Gilgamesh for help in taming Enkidu by sending a temple prostitute to civilize him.

Lines 79–100 The trapper followed his father's advice and went to Gilgamesh. Gilgamesh listened to the trapper's story and ordered him to take a prostitute named **Shamhat** to the watering hole where Enkidu lived. She would use her charms to bring Enkidu into the world of men.

Shamhat Civilizes Enkidu

Lines 101–140 The trapper and Shamhat traveled to the watering hole and waited for Enkidu to appear. When he arrived with the animals, Shamhat exposed herself to Enkidu. He was mesmerized by her beauty and approached her. They lay together for six days and seven nights.

After this, Enkidu returned to the animals, but they no longer accepted him. He had lost his innocence and wildness. Shamhat told Enkidu that he had become like a god and should now come with her to the city of Uruk, where Gilgamesh ruled.

Lines 141–170 Shamhat clothed Enkidu and led him to the city. Along the way, she taught him the ways of human life: eating bread, drinking wine, and wearing clothes. Enkidu was amazed by the new world he was entering.

Gilgamesh's Dreams

Lines 171–210 Meanwhile, Gilgamesh had dreams about a powerful companion who would soon come into his life. He dreamed of a star falling from the sky and a great axe. When he asked his mother, **Ninsun**, to interpret the dreams, she told him that a strong and faithful friend would soon arrive, someone who would be his equal and stand by his side.

Lines 211–240 Gilgamesh eagerly awaited this new companion, and the stage was set for the meeting between Gilgamesh and Enkidu, which would change both of their lives.

Analysis and Key Themes:

1. **Oppression of Gilgamesh**: The first tablet establishes Gilgamesh as a powerful, but tyrannical ruler whose unchecked strength and divine heritage lead him to exploit his people. The gods respond to the cries of the people by creating a counterpart, Enkidu, to balance Gilgamesh's excesses.
2. **Creation of Enkidu**: Enkidu's creation by the gods mirrors the creation of Adam in biblical texts or other myths. He begins as a wild, untamed force of nature, in harmony with the animals, but is transformed through his contact with Shamhat into a human who can confront Gilgamesh.
3. **Civilization vs. Nature**: Enkidu's transformation from a wild man into a civilized one raises questions about the nature of humanity and civilization. His sexual relationship with Shamhat marks the turning point where he becomes more

human and is separated from the natural world. This transition also suggests that civilization involves both the loss of innocence and the acquisition of knowledge and responsibility.
4. **Dreams and Prophecies**: Gilgamesh's dreams serve as a foreshadowing device, highlighting the importance of Enkidu's arrival. The dreams suggest that while Gilgamesh may have strength and power, he is still connected to the divine through his dreams and his mother, Ninsun, who helps interpret their meaning.

This is a direct translation and summation of the first tablet of the *Epic of Gilgamesh*. Different translations may vary slightly in wording, but the core narrative remains the same.

Tablet II of the *Epic of Gilgamesh* details the meeting of Enkidu and Gilgamesh, their initial confrontation, and the beginning of their deep friendship. Enkidu, after being civilized by Shamhat, journeys to Uruk, where he challenges Gilgamesh. Their battle transforms into a bond of mutual respect and loyalty. Below is a translation of the second tablet:

Tablet II: Enkidu and Gilgamesh Become Friends

Lines 1–40: Enkidu Enters Civilization

Enkidu, now fully clothed and having learned the ways of human life from Shamhat, sets out to enter the city of Uruk. As he walks with Shamhat, she tells him of Gilgamesh, the mighty king who is oppressive and rules his people harshly. She speaks of Gilgamesh's great strength, describing how he overworks the young men and takes the young women for himself.

Shamhat tells Enkidu, "He is Gilgamesh, supreme in strength. He leads the people like a shepherd, but his heart is too proud, and his rule too harsh. None can withstand his might, and he takes whatever he desires."

Enkidu, filled with righteous anger, decides to confront Gilgamesh. He wishes to challenge him and put an end to his oppressive rule over Uruk.

Lines 41–80: Enkidu Learns of Gilgamesh's Tyranny

On the journey to Uruk, Shamhat and Enkidu stop at a shepherd's camp. There, Enkidu is introduced to more elements of human life, including bread and wine. At first, he is hesitant, as he has only known wild foods, but Shamhat encourages him to partake. After eating and drinking, Enkidu feels stronger and more alert. He spends time with the shepherds, guarding their flocks and helping them with their daily work.

While with the shepherds, Enkidu learns more about Gilgamesh's behavior. The people of Uruk live in fear of their king, who exercises the *right of the first night* (a claim to sleep with brides before their husbands). Enkidu becomes enraged and resolves to stop Gilgamesh's abuses.

Lines 81–120: Enkidu Confronts Gilgamesh

Soon after, a messenger arrives to tell of an upcoming wedding in Uruk, where Gilgamesh intends to exercise his right. Hearing this, Enkidu rushes to the city. Upon entering Uruk, he blocks the path of Gilgamesh, preventing him from entering the bridal chamber. The two mighty men stand face to face, preparing for battle.

Gilgamesh, astonished by Enkidu's boldness, confronts him. The two engage in a fierce wrestling match that shakes the walls of Uruk. They fight with all their strength, but neither can gain a clear advantage over the other. The battle continues until, exhausted, Gilgamesh and Enkidu recognize each other's strength and relent.

Lines 121–170: The Bond of Friendship

After the battle, Gilgamesh and Enkidu embrace, their rivalry turning into mutual respect and friendship. Gilgamesh speaks to Enkidu, "You are the strongest of all men I have fought. You are like me, born of the wild but destined for greatness."

Enkidu, likewise, feels a deep connection to Gilgamesh. Though he was created to challenge him, he now sees in Gilgamesh a worthy companion, someone who shares his strength and spirit. They vow to become brothers, and together, they will accomplish great deeds.

Lines 171–210: Gilgamesh Proposes an Adventure

As their friendship grows, Gilgamesh feels a newfound sense of purpose. No longer satisfied with ruling over Uruk, he longs for adventure. He proposes that they journey together to the **Cedar Forest**, a distant land guarded by the fearsome monster **Humbaba**. There, they will make a name for themselves by defeating Humbaba and cutting down the sacred cedar trees.

Enkidu is hesitant at first, knowing that Humbaba is a terrifying creature protected by the god **Enlil**, but he ultimately agrees to join Gilgamesh. He warns Gilgamesh of the dangers, yet Gilgamesh, driven by a desire for glory, is undeterred.

Lines 211–250: Preparations for the Journey

Gilgamesh and Enkidu prepare for their journey to the Cedar Forest. They gather weapons and speak to the elders of Uruk, seeking their blessing and advice. The elders express concern about the dangers of the journey and advise Gilgamesh to rely on Enkidu's wisdom, as Enkidu knows the wild lands and the risks they present.

Gilgamesh's mother, **Ninsun**, also blesses the journey. She adopts Enkidu as a son, performing a ritual to bind the two together in friendship. Ninsun speaks to Shamash, the sun god, asking him to watch over her son and his companion on their perilous journey.

Themes and Key Moments:

1. **Civilization and the Transformation of Enkidu**: The first part of the tablet continues the theme of Enkidu's transformation from a wild man into a

member of human society. This transition is symbolized by his consumption of bread and wine, foods of civilization, as well as his gradual adoption of human customs. Through Shamhat, Enkidu is introduced to the complex world of human relationships, politics, and power dynamics.
2. **Confrontation with Gilgamesh**: The central moment of the tablet is the confrontation between Gilgamesh and Enkidu. The fight is more than a physical struggle; it symbolizes the balance between civilization and nature, and between unrestrained power (Gilgamesh) and natural justice (Enkidu). Their struggle leads to mutual respect, which marks the beginning of their deep friendship.
3. **Friendship and Brotherhood**: The bond that forms between Gilgamesh and Enkidu is one of the most significant themes in the epic. Their friendship is based on a recognition of each other's strength and character. Together, they complement each other—Gilgamesh's ambition and drive for fame are tempered by Enkidu's wisdom and understanding of nature. This friendship sets the stage for the rest of the epic.
4. **The Quest for Fame**: Gilgamesh's desire for adventure and to make a lasting name for himself is a key motivator in the epic. He sees his friendship with Enkidu as a means to achieve greater things, and their journey to confront Humbaba is his first step toward legendary status. This reflects a central theme of the epic—the pursuit of immortality through deeds that outlive one's physical life.
5. **The Role of the Gods**: The tablet also emphasizes the role of the gods in human affairs. Shamash, the sun god, is asked by Ninsun to protect Gilgamesh and Enkidu on their journey. The gods play an active role in shaping events and offering guidance,

showing the deep interconnection between the divine and human realms in Sumerian mythology.

This translation of **Tablet II** highlights the development of the key relationship between Gilgamesh and Enkidu and sets the stage for their epic adventures together. Their deepening bond not only drives the action of the story but also opens up larger themes about friendship, heroism, and mortality.

Tablet III of the *Epic of Gilgamesh* continues from where the second tablet left off, focusing on Gilgamesh and Enkidu's preparations for their dangerous journey to the Cedar Forest to confront the monstrous guardian, Humbaba. This tablet also highlights the relationship between Gilgamesh, Enkidu, and the elders of Uruk, as well as the role of Gilgamesh's mother, Ninsun, in blessing the journey.

Here is the translation of **Tablet III: Preparation for the Journey**:

Tablet III: Preparation for the Journey

Lines 1–20: Gilgamesh Declares His Intentions

Gilgamesh, eager to embark on his quest for glory, calls for a grand assembly of the people of Uruk. He addresses the city's elders, proclaiming his desire to journey to the Cedar Forest to slay the monstrous **Humbaba**, the guardian of the forest, who has been appointed by the god **Enlil**.

Gilgamesh tells the elders: "I will cut down the cedar trees, and I will make my name famous forever! Humbaba's terror must end, and I will be the one to do it. This is a journey that will bring great glory to Uruk."

Lines 21–40: The Elders' Advice

The elders of Uruk listen to Gilgamesh's plan with concern. They know of the dangers of the Cedar Forest and the ferocity of Humbaba. Humbaba's roar is said to be like the flood, his mouth is fire, and his breath is death. Despite this, Gilgamesh's determination is unwavering.

The elders offer him their advice: "Be cautious, Gilgamesh. Humbaba is a fearsome foe, and his strength is not to be underestimated. Trust in Enkidu, for he knows the wilderness and its dangers. Let Enkidu lead you, and rely on his wisdom as you go."

Gilgamesh accepts their counsel, but his resolve remains unchanged. He is focused on achieving a great name that will last for eternity.

Lines 41–80: The Blessing of Ninsun

Gilgamesh goes to visit his mother, the wise goddess **Ninsun**, to seek her blessing before the journey. Ninsun is deeply worried for her son, knowing that his quest is fraught with danger. She is aware that Humbaba is a powerful creature and that the journey is perilous.

Ninsun goes to the rooftop of her temple and makes offerings to the sun god, **Shamash**, asking for his protection over her son. She prays: "O Shamash, protector of travelers, guide my son in the dangerous forest, keep him safe, and bring him back to me."

After offering her prayers, Ninsun summons Enkidu. She performs a ritual in which she adopts Enkidu as her own son, thereby binding him spiritually to Gilgamesh. She speaks to Enkidu: "You are now my son, just as Gilgamesh is. Protect him as a brother, and stand by his side in the face of danger."

Lines 81–100: Gilgamesh and Enkidu Prepare for the Journey

With the blessings of his mother and the advice of the elders, Gilgamesh feels emboldened. He and Enkidu prepare for their departure, gathering weapons and provisions for the journey. They arm themselves with powerful axes and swords, knowing that the battle ahead will be fierce.

As they prepare, the people of Uruk watch with a mixture of awe and fear. They know that their king is embarking on a journey of great peril, but they also believe that his success could bring immense glory to the city.

Lines 101–140: The Final Farewell

Before they depart, Gilgamesh and Enkidu stand before the great gate of Uruk. The elders approach them one last time to offer their final words of wisdom.

The elders say to Gilgamesh: "Do not rely solely on your strength, great king. Trust in Enkidu, for he knows the ways of the wilderness. Enkidu must guide you through the Cedar Forest. May the gods watch over you both."

Gilgamesh thanks the elders and reassures them: "I will return to Uruk victorious. The name of Gilgamesh will be known throughout the lands!"

Lines 141–170: The Departure

With everything in place, Gilgamesh and Enkidu depart from Uruk. The people gather to watch them leave, offering prayers and well-wishes for their safe return. Gilgamesh strides ahead with confidence, and Enkidu walks beside him, ever watchful and ready for the challenges that lie ahead.

The journey to the Cedar Forest has begun.

Key Themes and Analysis:

1. **The Role of the Elders**: In this tablet, we see the importance of the elders of Uruk in providing wisdom and guidance. Although they warn Gilgamesh about the dangers of Humbaba and urge him to rely on Enkidu's knowledge of the wilderness, Gilgamesh's ambition drives him forward. The elders represent caution and

experience, while Gilgamesh represents youthful ambition and the desire for eternal glory.
2. **Ninsun's Blessing**: Gilgamesh's mother, Ninsun, plays a crucial role in offering divine protection through her prayer to Shamash, the sun god. Ninsun's ritual of adopting Enkidu as her son symbolizes the strengthening of the bond between Gilgamesh and Enkidu. By calling on Shamash, Ninsun ensures that her son's journey is under divine protection, reinforcing the idea that the gods are deeply involved in human affairs.
3. **Friendship and Brotherhood**: The ritual performed by Ninsun, in which she adopts Enkidu as her son, solidifies the brotherhood between Gilgamesh and Enkidu. They are no longer just companions; they are spiritually connected as brothers. This deep bond is central to the epic and sets the stage for the intense loyalty and friendship they will share.
4. **The Quest for Glory**: Gilgamesh's desire for fame and immortality is a driving force in this tablet. He believes that by defeating Humbaba and cutting down the cedar trees, he will achieve a lasting legacy. This theme of the pursuit of eternal glory, even in the face of extreme danger, will continue throughout the epic.
5. **The Role of the Gods**: The involvement of Shamash and Ninsun highlights the belief in divine intervention in human affairs. Ninsun's prayer to Shamash is an important moment, as it shows that the gods are both protectors and influencers of the journey. Gilgamesh's success is not only based on his strength but also on the favor of the gods.

This translation of **Tablet III** focuses on the preparations for the journey to the Cedar Forest, with a strong emphasis on the guidance of the elders, the blessing of Ninsun, and the deepening bond between Gilgamesh and Enkidu. The tablet sets the stage for the adventures that follow and the themes of friendship, heroism, and divine intervention that will define the epic.

Tablet IV of the *Epic of Gilgamesh*, titled "The Journey to the Cedar Forest," describes the long and perilous journey undertaken by Gilgamesh and Enkidu to reach the Cedar Forest, home of the monstrous guardian, Humbaba. This tablet emphasizes their growing friendship, the challenges they face, and the ominous dreams that Gilgamesh has along the way.

Here is a translation of **Tablet IV: The Journey to the Cedar Forest**:

Tablet IV: The Journey to the Cedar Forest

Lines 1–20: Setting Out on the Journey

Gilgamesh and Enkidu set off from Uruk on their journey toward the Cedar Forest, determined to defeat **Humbaba** and bring glory to their names. They walk side by side, carrying their weapons: axes, swords, and bows. As they travel, they pass through vast, unknown territories—plains, hills, and mountains.

They walk twenty leagues in the first day and stop for the night. Gilgamesh digs a well to offer water to the gods and prays for their protection on this dangerous quest.

Lines 21–50: Gilgamesh's First Dream

That night, as they rest, Gilgamesh has a dream. He awakens and tells Enkidu, "I had a dream. The mountain fell on me, trapping me. It was as though the sky and the earth were bound together. Everything was darkness, and I could not move."

Enkidu interprets the dream for him, reassuring Gilgamesh: "Your dream is a good omen. The mountain you saw represents Humbaba. It means that we will defeat him, and your fame will reach the heavens."

Reassured by Enkidu's interpretation, Gilgamesh feels emboldened and confident once more.

Lines 51–80: Continuing the Journey

The two heroes continue their journey the next day, walking another twenty leagues. They travel through the wilderness, crossing rivers and forests, drawing closer to the Cedar Forest. As before, they stop to rest for the night, and Gilgamesh once again offers water to the gods in prayer.

That night, Gilgamesh has another dream.

Lines 81–110: Gilgamesh's Second Dream

In this second dream, Gilgamesh sees something terrible. He says to Enkidu: "In my dream, I saw a great bull. It was charging at me, snorting, and kicking up dust. Then it pinned me down and held me in its grasp, but I managed to overcome it."

Enkidu once again interprets the dream. He explains: "The bull represents Shamash, the sun god, who is your protector on this journey. It means that Shamash will aid us in our battle, and we will prevail against Humbaba."

With renewed determination, Gilgamesh continues on, trusting in Enkidu's wisdom and the protection of Shamash.

Lines 111–150: The Third Day of Travel

On the third day, they journey further into the wilderness, covering another twenty leagues. They stop at sunset and prepare to rest once more. Gilgamesh digs another well to offer water to the gods and asks for their continued protection.

That night, Gilgamesh has another dream, this one even more troubling than the last.

Lines 151–180: Gilgamesh's Third Dream

In his third dream, Gilgamesh sees the earth shaking, and fire and smoke fill the air. He tells Enkidu: "In my dream, the earth was trembling, and fire rained down from the sky. Everything was consumed by flames, and there was no escape."

Enkidu interprets the dream again: "Do not fear, my brother. The fire you saw represents the power of Humbaba, but it also shows that we will overcome him. The gods are with us, and they will ensure our victory."

Despite the unsettling nature of his dreams, Gilgamesh feels reassured by Enkidu's interpretations and presses forward.

Lines 181–210: The Fourth Day of Travel

On the fourth day of their journey, Gilgamesh and Enkidu reach the foothills of the Cedar Forest. They can smell the scent of the cedars on the air and know that they are close. The dense forest looms before them, dark and mysterious.

Once again, they stop for the night. Gilgamesh performs his ritual of offering water to the gods and prays for protection as they prepare to enter the Cedar Forest.

Lines 211–240: Gilgamesh's Fourth Dream

Gilgamesh has one final dream before they enter the forest. He dreams of a fierce storm, with lightning flashing and thunder roaring. He tells Enkidu: "In my dream, a great storm came. The winds howled, and the sky was filled with lightning. The ground trembled, and the storm was overwhelming."

Enkidu interprets this dream as well: "The storm is a sign of the power of the gods. It is a good omen. The storm represents the might of Shamash, and it means that the gods will support us in our battle against Humbaba. We will triumph."

With this final dream, Gilgamesh feels prepared for the challenges ahead.

Lines 241–270: Approaching the Cedar Forest

Gilgamesh and Enkidu, now strengthened by the dreams and reassured by the gods' protection, approach the Cedar Forest with caution. The towering trees cast long shadows, and the forest itself feels alive, as if it is watching them.

Enkidu, having known the wilderness, advises Gilgamesh: "Be on guard, for this is the domain of Humbaba. His power is great, and the gods have appointed him to guard this sacred forest. But with the help of Shamash, we will prevail."

Together, they prepare to face the mighty Humbaba.

Key Themes and Analysis:

1. **Dreams as Omens**: The recurring dreams that Gilgamesh experiences are significant in ancient Mesopotamian culture, as dreams were believed to be messages from the gods. Gilgamesh's dreams throughout this tablet serve as premonitions of the battle to come. Enkidu's interpretations consistently reassure Gilgamesh that the dreams are favorable,

providing both of them with confidence and the belief that they are under divine protection.
2. **Enkidu's Role as a Guide**: Throughout this tablet, Enkidu plays the role of both companion and guide. His knowledge of the wilderness, his wisdom in interpreting dreams, and his calm demeanor help Gilgamesh navigate both the physical and psychological challenges of their journey. Enkidu's familiarity with the natural world and its dangers complements Gilgamesh's strength and ambition.
3. **Divine Intervention and Protection**: The presence of the gods, particularly **Shamash**, is felt throughout the journey. Gilgamesh and Enkidu consistently offer prayers and perform rituals to gain the favor and protection of the gods. The dreams suggest that Shamash will play an important role in their success against Humbaba, reinforcing the idea that the heroes' fate is closely intertwined with the will of the gods.
4. **The Journey as a Rite of Passage**: The long journey to the Cedar Forest serves as a rite of passage for Gilgamesh. Each day of travel brings physical and emotional challenges, and the dreams he experiences along the way reflect his fears and uncertainties. By overcoming these challenges, both Gilgamesh and Enkidu grow stronger and more confident, preparing themselves for the monumental battle ahead.
5. **The Power of Nature**: The forest itself, and the natural world around it, is portrayed as both beautiful and dangerous. The Cedar Forest, guarded by Humbaba, represents the untamed forces of nature that Gilgamesh seeks to conquer. The dreams of storms, earthquakes, and fire reflect the overwhelming power of the natural world, a power

that Gilgamesh must contend with in his quest for glory.

This translation of **Tablet IV** emphasizes the development of the journey to the Cedar Forest, the growing bond between Gilgamesh and Enkidu, and the significant role of dreams and divine intervention. As they approach their goal, both heroes are tested in mind and body, preparing for the confrontation with Humbaba, the fearsome guardian of the forest.

Tablet V of the *Epic of Gilgamesh*, titled "The Battle with Humbaba," narrates the dramatic encounter between Gilgamesh, Enkidu, and the fearsome guardian of the Cedar Forest, Humbaba (also known as Huwawa). In this tablet, Gilgamesh and Enkidu confront the monster, aided by the divine powers of the sun god Shamash. The tablet explores themes of courage, divine intervention, and the nature of good and evil.

Here is a translation of **Tablet V: The Battle with Humbaba**:

Tablet V: The Battle with Humbaba

Lines 1–30: Entering the Cedar Forest

Gilgamesh and Enkidu stand at the entrance to the **Cedar Forest**, marveling at its immense beauty. The trees are towering and thick, and the scent of cedar fills the air. The forest is the realm of the gods, a sacred place guarded by the monstrous Humbaba, appointed by **Enlil**, the god of earth, wind, and air.

The two heroes take a moment to admire the splendor of the forest, but they know the danger that lies ahead. They begin their approach into the dense woods, walking cautiously. The earth trembles beneath their feet, as though alive with the presence of Humbaba.

Lines 31–60: Humbaba's First Appearance

As they venture deeper into the forest, they hear the sound of Humbaba's footsteps approaching. The ground shakes, and the air becomes thick with a terrifying presence. Suddenly, **Humbaba** emerges, roaring like a thunderstorm. His face is terrifying, and he radiates an overwhelming aura of fear and death. His mouth spews fire, and his breath is like death itself.

Gilgamesh and Enkidu are momentarily struck with fear. Humbaba, seeing them, speaks with rage: "Who dares to enter my forest? I have been appointed by Enlil to guard these sacred trees. No mortal may trespass here!"

Enkidu urges Gilgamesh to stand firm and not to show fear, reminding him of their mission. Gilgamesh, with his courage renewed, raises his weapons and calls out to Humbaba, challenging him to battle.

Lines 61–90: The Battle Begins

The battle between the two heroes and Humbaba begins. Gilgamesh and Enkidu attack together, but Humbaba's power is immense. He roars with fury, and the trees shake at his command. The winds howl, and the ground trembles as Humbaba unleashes his strength. His blows are like hurricanes, and his speed is terrifying.

Despite their bravery, Gilgamesh and Enkidu struggle against the sheer power of the monster. They fight valiantly but are pushed back, nearly overwhelmed by his force. Gilgamesh calls upon **Shamash**, the sun god, for aid, asking for divine intervention to defeat this fearsome enemy.

Lines 91–120: Shamash's Intervention

Shamash hears Gilgamesh's prayer and answers by sending powerful winds to bind Humbaba. The winds come from all directions—north, south, east, and west—pinning Humbaba in place. The winds prevent him from moving freely, weakening his strength and giving Gilgamesh and Enkidu the advantage they need.

Seeing Humbaba trapped by the winds, Gilgamesh and Enkidu press their attack. Humbaba, now vulnerable, pleads for his life. He cries out to Gilgamesh, "I know you are strong and favored by the gods. Spare me, and I will serve you. I will cut down the cedar trees for you and build a great palace. You do not need to kill me to win glory!"

Lines 121–150: Enkidu's Counsel and Humbaba's Death

Gilgamesh hesitates, moved by Humbaba's plea for mercy. He considers sparing the monster, thinking perhaps there is honor in showing compassion. But **Enkidu** intervenes, reminding Gilgamesh of their mission and the threat that Humbaba poses to the world.

Enkidu speaks: "Do not listen to his words, Gilgamesh. Humbaba is a servant of Enlil, and he cannot be trusted. If you spare him, he will rise again, more powerful and vengeful. Finish the task we set out to do. Strike him down now and make your name eternal!"

Gilgamesh, convinced by Enkidu's words, raises his axe and delivers the fatal blow to Humbaba. The monster falls, defeated, and the two heroes rejoice in their victory. With Humbaba's death, the great Cedar Forest is free from his terror.

Lines 151–180: The Aftermath of the Battle

After the battle, Gilgamesh and Enkidu look upon the slain body of Humbaba. They feel both triumph and a sense of sorrow. Although they have won a great victory, they realize that they have destroyed a powerful being who had served the gods.

They begin to cut down the sacred cedar trees, as they had planned. Gilgamesh selects the tallest and finest of the trees to build a great gate for the city of Uruk. He also intends to use the cedar wood to build a mighty temple in honor of the gods.

Lines 181–210: Enlil's Wrath

As Gilgamesh and Enkidu celebrate their victory, they are struck by a deep foreboding. The death of Humbaba has not gone unnoticed by the gods. **Enlil**, who had appointed Humbaba to guard the Cedar Forest, is enraged by the death of his servant.

Though the heroes have achieved their goal, they realize that they have also defied the will of Enlil, one of the most powerful gods in the pantheon. They know that the consequences of this action may still be felt in the future.

With the cedar trees in tow, Gilgamesh and Enkidu begin their journey back to Uruk, aware that their victory, though glorious, has also set in motion forces that they cannot control.

Key Themes and Analysis:

1. **The Nature of Heroism**: Gilgamesh's battle with Humbaba is a classic test of heroism, where strength, courage, and divine favor are all needed to overcome a formidable foe. However, the tablet also explores the complexity of heroism, especially in Gilgamesh's hesitation to kill Humbaba. The tension between mercy and duty is a significant theme, as Gilgamesh grapples with whether to show compassion or fulfill his mission.
2. **Divine Intervention**: The role of Shamash is central to the heroes' success in defeating Humbaba. The winds sent by Shamash are a clear indication that the gods are involved in human affairs, and without Shamash's help, Gilgamesh and Enkidu would likely have been defeated. The tablet emphasizes that even the greatest heroes cannot achieve their goals without the favor of the gods.

3. **Enkidu as a Moral Guide**: Enkidu plays a critical role in this tablet as a moral and practical guide for Gilgamesh. While Gilgamesh is swayed by Humbaba's pleas for mercy, Enkidu remains focused on the task at hand. His advice to Gilgamesh—to kill Humbaba and not show mercy—shows that Enkidu understands the long-term consequences of allowing the monster to live. He emphasizes the need for decisive action in the face of evil.
4. **The Power of Nature and the Gods**: Humbaba's control over the Cedar Forest and his immense power represent the untamed forces of nature, which are protected by the gods. By defeating Humbaba, Gilgamesh and Enkidu challenge the gods themselves, particularly Enlil, the god of the earth. This victory over a divine servant foreshadows the heroes' future struggles with the gods, as their defiance may bring about divine retribution.
5. **Victory and Sorrow**: The tablet ends with a mixed sense of triumph and sorrow. While Gilgamesh and Enkidu have achieved their goal, the act of killing Humbaba—a creature appointed by the gods—comes with a sense of unease. They realize that their actions may have angered the gods, particularly Enlil, and this sets the stage for the eventual consequences of their defiance.

This translation of **Tablet V** highlights the intense battle with Humbaba and the significant moral and emotional complexities faced by Gilgamesh and Enkidu. Their victory, while glorious, is also tinged with the recognition that their actions may have far-reaching consequences in the world of the gods.

Epic of Gilgamesh, titled "Ishtar and the Bull of Heaven," tells the story of the goddess Ishtar's attempt to seduce Gilgamesh, his rejection of her advances, and the deadly consequences of this rejection. In response to the humiliation, Ishtar unleashes the **Bull of Heaven** to punish Gilgamesh and the people of Uruk. This tablet explores themes of divine power, human defiance, and the relationship between gods and mortals.

Here is a translation of **Tablet VI: Ishtar and the Bull of Heaven**:

Tablet VI: Ishtar and the Bull of Heaven

Lines 1–30: Ishtar's Proposal to Gilgamesh

After Gilgamesh and Enkidu return to the city of Uruk, victorious from their battle with Humbaba, Gilgamesh cleanses himself, dons his royal garments, and wears his crown. His beauty and strength catch the attention of **Ishtar**, the goddess of love, fertility, and war.

Ishtar approaches Gilgamesh, filled with desire, and proposes marriage to him. She says to Gilgamesh, "Come, Gilgamesh, be my husband. I will offer you riches beyond imagination. I will give you a chariot of lapis lazuli and gold, and you will be drawn by powerful lions. Kings and princes will bow before you, and your herds and crops will prosper under my favor."

Lines 31–60: Gilgamesh Rejects Ishtar

Gilgamesh, however, is wary of Ishtar's notorious reputation for treating her lovers cruelly after winning their affection. He responds to her proposal with scorn, listing the fates of her previous lovers:

"Which of your lovers did you ever love forever? Your love is fleeting. You loved **Tammuz**, the shepherd, and condemned him to the underworld. You loved a lion and caused him to be mauled in a pit. You loved a stallion and doomed him to endless running and thirst. You loved a shepherd bird and broke its wing.

Why should I be any different? I know how you treat those who love you. You bring ruin to those who accept your love."

Lines 61–90: Ishtar's Rage

Hearing this, Ishtar is furious. Humiliated by Gilgamesh's rejection and stinging from his harsh words, she flies into a rage. She ascends to the heavens to speak with her father, **Anu**, the god of the sky, and her mother, **Antum**.

Ishtar cries to Anu, "Father, Gilgamesh has insulted me! He has spoken harshly of me and rejected my love. Give me the **Bull of Heaven** so that I may punish him and destroy his city. If you do not grant me this request, I will unleash the dead from the underworld, and they will outnumber the living. The world will be overrun with the dead!"

Lines 91–120: The Bull of Heaven Unleashed

Anu is hesitant at first, warning Ishtar that unleashing the Bull of Heaven will cause severe destruction on earth. However, Ishtar persists, and Anu eventually gives in to her demands. He gives her the reins of the **Bull of Heaven** and tells her to release it upon Uruk.

Ishtar descends to earth, leading the Bull of Heaven to the city of Uruk. As the bull descends, the earth trembles. The Bull's first roar opens a massive chasm in the ground, swallowing a hundred men of Uruk. The Bull roars a second time, creating another chasm that devours two hundred men.

Lines 121–150: The Battle with the Bull of Heaven

Gilgamesh and Enkidu see the destruction caused by the Bull of Heaven and rush to defend their city. Enkidu grabs the bull by its horns, and with great strength, he forces it to a standstill. He calls out to Gilgamesh: "My friend, strike now while I hold the bull!"

Gilgamesh, seizing the opportunity, draws his sword and plunges it into the neck of the Bull of Heaven, delivering a fatal blow. The mighty creature falls dead, and the people of Uruk rejoice at the victory of their king and his companion.

Lines 151–180: Ishtar's Grief and Enkidu's Mockery

Upon seeing the Bull of Heaven slain, Ishtar climbs to the top of the walls of Uruk. She wails in sorrow and curses Gilgamesh and Enkidu, furious at the death of the sacred bull that she had brought to punish them.

Enkidu, filled with anger and defiance, taunts Ishtar. He tears off the **thigh** of the Bull of Heaven and hurls it toward her, saying, "If I could reach you, I would treat you as I have treated this bull. Your threats and curses mean nothing to us!"

Ishtar, humiliated once again, retreats to her temple, where her priestesses gather in mourning for the Bull of Heaven.

Lines 181–210: Gilgamesh and Enkidu's Celebration

After their victory, Gilgamesh and Enkidu return to the palace of Uruk, where they are greeted with celebration. The people of Uruk honor them for saving the city from destruction. Gilgamesh holds a grand feast in his palace to celebrate their triumph over the Bull of Heaven.

During the feast, Gilgamesh and Enkidu offer praise to the gods, particularly Shamash, who had guided them on their journey. They rejoice in their strength and bravery, boasting of their victories against both Humbaba and the Bull of Heaven.

Lines 211–230: The Gods' Judgment

However, the gods are not pleased with the death of the Bull of Heaven. In the divine assembly, the gods meet to discuss the actions of Gilgamesh and Enkidu. **Anu**, **Enlil**, and **Shamash** gather to decide the fate of the two heroes.

Enlil, angered by the death of the Bull of Heaven and the defiance of Gilgamesh and Enkidu, declares that one of the two must be punished for these offenses. Shamash, who has supported Gilgamesh and Enkidu, argues in their defense, but Enlil's will is final.

It is decided that **Enkidu** must pay for these transgressions with his life.

Key Themes and Analysis:

1. **Divine Power and Human Defiance**: This tablet explores the dangerous consequences of challenging the gods. Gilgamesh's rejection of Ishtar, a powerful goddess, leads to the unleashing of the Bull of Heaven, demonstrating the gods' ability to punish mortals who defy them. However, Gilgamesh and Enkidu's ability to kill the bull shows that humans can confront divine powers, though there are consequences for such actions.
2. **Ishtar's Wrath**: Ishtar, as a goddess of love and war, embodies both the nurturing and destructive aspects of divinity. Her anger at being rejected by Gilgamesh highlights the volatile nature of the gods in Mesopotamian mythology. Ishtar's vindictiveness drives the plot forward,

demonstrating how the whims of gods can drastically affect human lives.

3. **Enkidu as a Symbol of Defiance**: Enkidu's role in mocking Ishtar after the death of the Bull of Heaven reflects his bold defiance of the gods. His action of throwing the thigh of the bull at Ishtar is a significant moment of rebellion, symbolizing the growing tension between mortals and the divine. This act, however, foreshadows his eventual punishment.
4. **The Role of Fate**: The gods' decision to punish Enkidu for the slaying of the Bull of Heaven reflects the inescapable role of fate in the epic. Despite their victories and bravery, Gilgamesh and Enkidu cannot escape the judgment of the gods. This sets the stage for Enkidu's tragic fate in the following tablets.
5. **The Fragility of Glory**: Gilgamesh and Enkidu's victory over the Bull of Heaven is a moment of triumph, but it is short-lived. The celebration in Uruk contrasts with the divine judgment that follows, reminding the reader that human glory is fleeting and that even the greatest heroes are subject to the will of the gods.

This translation of **Tablet VI** highlights the complex relationships between gods and mortals in the *Epic of Gilgamesh*. The tablet explores the consequences of defying the divine, setting the stage for the tragic events that will follow in the subsequent tablets, particularly the punishment of Enkidu.

Tablet VII of the *Epic of Gilgamesh*, titled "The Death of Enkidu," is one of the most emotionally charged sections of the epic. In this tablet, Enkidu dreams of the gods decreeing his death as punishment for killing the Bull of Heaven and Humbaba. Enkidu falls ill, reflects on his life and friendship with Gilgamesh, and ultimately dies. This tablet sets the stage for Gilgamesh's profound grief and his later quest for immortality.

Here is a translation of **Tablet VII: The Death of Enkidu**:

Tablet VII: The Death of Enkidu

Lines 1–40: Enkidu's Ominous Dream

After their victory over the Bull of Heaven, Enkidu begins to have troubling dreams. In his sleep, he is tormented by visions sent by the gods. One night, he wakes up in terror and tells Gilgamesh about a dream he had.

Enkidu says, "In my dream, the gods were angry. They sat in counsel, and **Anu**, **Enlil**, **Ea**, and **Shamash** gathered to decide our fate. Anu spoke: 'Because they killed the Bull of Heaven and Humbaba, one of them must die.' Enlil agreed and declared that I must be the one to die."

Enkidu trembles with fear as he recounts the dream to Gilgamesh. He feels betrayed by the gods and overwhelmed by the inevitability of his fate.

Lines 41–70: Enkidu's Curse

Enkidu falls ill shortly after the dream. As the sickness worsens, he curses the day he left the wilderness and entered the world of humans. He curses **Shamhat**, the temple prostitute who first tamed him, for bringing him into civilization and setting him on this path of death.

"Cursed be Shamhat," Enkidu cries. "May she have no joy in her life, and may her beauty fade. It was she who led me away from the wild animals, from the simple life I knew, and brought me to this fate. I was once free with the gazelles and the wild beasts, but now I am doomed to die."

Enkidu's bitterness and anger reflect his deep sorrow over the loss of his former life and the realization that his time is running out.

Lines 71–120: Shamash's Reassurance

The sun god **Shamash**, hearing Enkidu's curses, speaks to him from the heavens. Shamash reminds Enkidu of the blessings he has experienced in his life since coming into contact with humanity.

"Enkidu, why do you curse Shamhat?" Shamash asks. "It was she who brought you into the world of humans, where you found friendship with Gilgamesh, and together you achieved great deeds. You became a hero and defeated the monsters Humbaba and the Bull of Heaven. You are remembered in glory, and you have known the love of a true friend."

Hearing Shamash's words, Enkidu's anger softens. He realizes that his time with Gilgamesh, though short, has been filled with meaningful moments. He acknowledges that he was blessed to have experienced the depth of friendship and the honor of heroic deeds.

Lines 121–150: Enkidu's Lament for His Life

Despite Shamash's reassurances, Enkidu is heartbroken over his impending death. He reflects on the life he has led and the joy he once knew as a wild man, roaming free in the wilderness. He regrets the path that led him to this point, feeling cheated by the gods.

He says, "Had I stayed with the wild beasts, I would not know this sorrow. I would not fear death as I do now. My heart aches, and my body weakens. I grieve for the life I once had, free from the troubles of men."

Enkidu's lament reveals his struggle to come to terms with mortality. His illness weighs heavily on him, both physically and emotionally, and he feels powerless against the will of the gods.

Lines 151–200: Enkidu's Farewell to Gilgamesh

As his condition worsens, Enkidu calls out to Gilgamesh. He tells his friend, "I grieve, Gilgamesh, because I know that I will die. I have seen the fate that awaits me. I will not return to the land of the living. I must go to the House of Dust, where the dead dwell, and there is no escape."

Gilgamesh, devastated by Enkidu's words, tries to comfort his friend, but he knows that there is nothing he can do to stop the gods' decree. He stays by Enkidu's side, holding his hand as his friend weakens.

Enkidu continues to speak of the underworld, describing it as a dark and dreary place: "The House of Dust is a place where the dead eat clay and are clothed in feathers. It is a realm of shadows, where kings, priests, and commoners alike are equal. The gods of the underworld are harsh, and once you enter, you cannot return."

Enkidu's fear of death and the underworld is palpable. He dreads the loneliness and isolation of the afterlife, leaving behind his friend and the world he has come to know.

Lines 201–230: Enkidu's Death

After twelve days of suffering, Enkidu dies. His final words are filled with sorrow for leaving Gilgamesh behind: "You were like a brother to me, Gilgamesh. Together, we accomplished great things, but now I must leave you."

With those words, Enkidu breathes his last breath.

Gilgamesh is left to mourn the loss of his closest friend. His grief is profound, and he weeps bitterly over Enkidu's body. He paces back and forth, tearing at his hair and clothes, unable to accept that his friend is gone.

Lines 231–270: Gilgamesh's Grief

Gilgamesh is overwhelmed by the finality of death. He cries out to the gods, cursing the fate that has taken Enkidu from him. His sorrow turns to fear, as he realizes that death will one day come for him as well. The loss of Enkidu forces Gilgamesh to confront his own mortality.

He speaks to Enkidu's lifeless body: "How can I bear this, my brother? You were the strong one, and now you are gone. Death has taken you, and I cannot follow. What am I to do without you?"

Gilgamesh calls upon the mountains and the wilderness, the places where they once journeyed together, to mourn Enkidu's passing. He orders the people of Uruk to grieve for Enkidu, and he vows to honor his friend's memory.

Key Themes and Analysis:

1. **The Inevitability of Death**: This tablet focuses heavily on the theme of mortality. Enkidu's illness and eventual death serve as a stark reminder to both Gilgamesh and the reader that death is an inescapable part of life. Enkidu's transformation from a wild, free man to a hero, and finally to a dying mortal, highlights the fragility of human existence.

2. **Friendship and Loss**: The deep bond between Gilgamesh and Enkidu is central to this tablet. Their friendship, which has been a source of strength and joy, becomes a source of immense sorrow as Enkidu nears death. Gilgamesh's grief reflects the profound impact that losing a loved one can have, and his fear of death is magnified by the loss of his closest companion.
3. **The House of Dust**: Enkidu's description of the afterlife as the "House of Dust" provides insight into the Mesopotamian view of death. The afterlife is depicted as a bleak and joyless place, where all souls, regardless of their status in life, are equal in their suffering. This grim portrayal of the underworld adds to Enkidu's fear of dying.
4. **Cursing and Acceptance**: Enkidu's initial reaction to his illness is one of anger and bitterness. He curses Shamhat for bringing him into the world of men, blaming her for his fate. However, after hearing Shamash's words, Enkidu begins to accept his fate, recognizing the blessings he experienced through his friendship with Gilgamesh. This transition from anger to acceptance is a key part of Enkidu's journey in this tablet.
5. **Gilgamesh's Confrontation with Mortality**: Enkidu's death is a turning point for Gilgamesh. Until this moment, Gilgamesh had been focused on achieving glory and greatness. However, Enkidu's death forces Gilgamesh to confront the reality of his own mortality, leading to his later quest for immortality. The fear of death, which was once distant, now becomes very real to him.

This translation of **Tablet VII** captures the emotional weight of Enkidu's death and its impact on both Enkidu and Gilgamesh. The themes of mortality, friendship, and the fear of the afterlife are central to this part of the epic, setting the stage for Gilgamesh's journey in the subsequent tablets, where he seeks to understand and possibly overcome death.

Tablet VIII of the *Epic of Gilgamesh*, titled "The Mourning of Gilgamesh," focuses on Gilgamesh's profound grief following the death of his closest friend, Enkidu. In this tablet, Gilgamesh mourns over Enkidu's body, expresses his sorrow, and prepares for the burial rites. Gilgamesh's sorrow serves as a key turning point, transitioning him from a hero seeking glory to a man deeply shaken by the reality of death.

Here is a translation of **Tablet VIII: The Mourning of Gilgamesh**:

Tablet VIII: The Mourning of Gilgamesh

Lines 1–20: Gilgamesh's Lament

After Enkidu dies, Gilgamesh is inconsolable. He weeps and mourns over the body of his friend, unable to accept that Enkidu is gone. He calls out in sorrow, "O Enkidu, my brother! You were the axe at my side, the sword in my hand, the shield before me. You were my companion in all things. How can you be gone?"

Gilgamesh's heart is filled with anguish. He wanders around the body of Enkidu, lamenting the loss of the bond they shared, the adventures they undertook together, and the joy they once experienced.

Lines 21–40: Calling the Wilderness to Mourn

In his grief, Gilgamesh calls upon all of nature to mourn the death of Enkidu. He invokes the hills, the rivers, the animals, and the fields to share in his sorrow. He calls to the creatures of the wilderness, the gazelles, the panthers, and the beasts that Enkidu once ran with, to mourn for him.

"O wild creatures of the forest, mourn for my friend, for he is gone. He who drank with you at the waterholes, who ran with you in the plains, is no more."

The wilderness, which had once been Enkidu's home, is summoned by Gilgamesh to join in his mourning. The imagery reflects the deep connection between Enkidu and the natural world, which now feels the weight of his absence.

Lines 41–60: Summoning the People to Grieve

Gilgamesh does not stop with the natural world; he also calls upon the people of Uruk to share in his grief. He orders that the craftsmen, the elders, and the young men and women of Uruk mourn for Enkidu.

"O people of Uruk, weep for my friend! The one who was mighty and strong, who fought alongside me, has been taken by death. Let all of Uruk grieve for him, for there will never be another like him."

Gilgamesh's sorrow is so great that he wants the entire city of Uruk to feel the loss that he feels. He wants the people to understand the greatness of Enkidu and the depth of the friendship they shared.

Lines 61–90: Preparing Enkidu for Burial

Unable to bear the sight of Enkidu's body as it lies lifeless before him, Gilgamesh prepares his friend for the journey to the underworld. He covers Enkidu's body in a great shroud, as is the custom, and prepares the finest offerings for his burial.

"I will make offerings to the gods on your behalf, my friend. I will place precious gifts beside you, and I will lay you to rest with the finest of honors. I will build a great statue of you in gold, so that your memory will never fade."

Gilgamesh ensures that Enkidu's passage to the afterlife is marked with the highest honor. He intends to preserve Enkidu's memory in the form of a grand statue, ensuring that the people of Uruk will remember his friend for generations.

Lines 91–120: The Offerings to the Gods

Gilgamesh calls for offerings to be made to the gods who dwell in the underworld. He makes offerings to **Namtar**, the god of death, to **Ereshkigal**, the queen of the underworld, and to **Nergal**, the god of war and death.

"May the gods of the underworld receive you well, my friend. May they welcome you with open arms, for you were a great and mighty warrior. I offer these gifts in your honor, so that you may find peace in the House of Dust."

Gilgamesh's offerings are meant to ease Enkidu's journey into the afterlife. He wants to ensure that his friend is treated well by the gods who rule the underworld, even though he is devastated by the thought of Enkidu's spirit departing from him forever.

Lines 121–150: Gilgamesh's Grief Intensifies

As the preparations for Enkidu's burial continue, Gilgamesh's grief only deepens. He refuses to accept that his friend is truly gone, and he cannot bear the thought of life without him. He speaks to Enkidu's lifeless body:

"Why, O Enkidu, did you have to leave me? Why did you abandon me to face this sorrow alone? My heart is broken, for you were my brother. You were the one who stood by me through all our battles, and now you are gone."

Gilgamesh's pain is overwhelming. He feels lost without his companion, and the realization that he, too, will one day face death fills him with fear and dread.

Lines 151–180: The Funeral Procession

Finally, the day of Enkidu's burial arrives. Gilgamesh leads a grand funeral procession through the streets of Uruk. The people of the city weep for Enkidu, as they follow their king in mourning.

Gilgamesh places Enkidu's body in the tomb, along with the offerings and treasures he has prepared. He orders the craftsmen of Uruk to build a great monument in honor of Enkidu, so that his memory will live on forever.

As the tomb is sealed, Gilgamesh cries out one last time for his friend: "Farewell, O Enkidu, my brother. May you find peace in the land of the dead. You will be remembered always, for you were the greatest of men."

Key Themes and Analysis:

1. **Grief and Loss**: The tablet centers on Gilgamesh's profound grief following Enkidu's death. Gilgamesh's sorrow is all-consuming, and the depth of his mourning shows the deep bond between the two. His lamentation over Enkidu's body reflects his emotional devastation and the sharp pain of losing a close friend.
2. **Mourning in Nature**: Gilgamesh's call for the wilderness and animals to mourn for Enkidu emphasizes Enkidu's connection to nature, which was a central part of his character. Gilgamesh's plea for the natural world to grieve reflects how deeply Enkidu's death impacts not only Gilgamesh but the entire world, including the wild animals that Enkidu once lived with.
3. **The Ritual of Death**: The tablet provides insight into the ancient Mesopotamian customs surrounding death and burial. Gilgamesh's meticulous preparations for Enkidu's funeral—covering him in a shroud, making offerings to the gods, and building a grand statue—demonstrate the importance of honoring the dead and ensuring they are properly cared for in the afterlife.
4. **Immortality Through Memory**: Gilgamesh's decision to build a statue of Enkidu symbolizes his desire to immortalize his friend's memory. By constructing a monument in his honor, Gilgamesh ensures that Enkidu's name will not be forgotten. This act of creating a lasting legacy foreshadows Gilgamesh's own fear of death and his later quest for immortality.

5. **The Realization of Mortality**: Enkidu's death marks the first time that Gilgamesh must confront his own mortality. The loss of his friend forces him to realize that even the mightiest of heroes cannot escape death. This realization will drive Gilgamesh to seek a way to overcome death, a theme that becomes central in the subsequent tablets.

This translation of **Tablet VIII** captures Gilgamesh's deep mourning for Enkidu and the grand funeral he arranges for his friend. The themes of grief, mortality, and the desire for remembrance are central to this part of the epic, as Gilgamesh begins to grapple with the idea of death and the impermanence of life.

Tablet IX of the *Epic of Gilgamesh*, titled "The Quest for Immortality," follows Gilgamesh as he embarks on a journey to seek eternal life after the death of his closest friend, Enkidu. Shaken by the reality of mortality, Gilgamesh, in his grief and fear, sets out to find **Utnapishtim**, a man who was granted immortality by the gods after surviving a great flood. Gilgamesh's quest takes him into unknown lands, as he seeks to escape death and gain knowledge of immortality.

Here is a translation of **Tablet IX: The Quest for Immortality**:

Tablet IX: The Quest for Immortality

Lines 1–30: Gilgamesh's Grief and Fear of Death

After Enkidu's death, Gilgamesh is consumed with grief and fear. He cannot stop mourning the loss of his friend and is haunted by the reality that he, too, will one day die. Gilgamesh, once confident and powerful, now feels vulnerable in the face of death.

He speaks to himself: "How can I be at peace? Death has taken Enkidu, and one day it will come for me as well. I am afraid of death, and I cannot bear the thought of being forgotten. Must I, too, die like all men? No, I will not accept it!"

Determined to escape the fate that awaits all mortals, Gilgamesh sets out on a journey to find **Utnapishtim**, the only man who has been granted eternal life by the gods. Gilgamesh believes that if he can find Utnapishtim, he will learn the secret to immortality.

Lines 31–60: The Journey Begins

Gilgamesh leaves the city of Uruk and travels alone into the wilderness. He crosses vast plains, climbs towering mountains, and traverses dangerous landscapes. His journey takes him farther than any man has ever gone, driven by his fear of death.

He speaks aloud: "I will find Utnapishtim, the Faraway. He is the one who knows the secret of life everlasting. I will go to the ends of the earth, if necessary, to escape death."

Gilgamesh travels for days and nights, covering vast distances. He is weary but determined, knowing that this is his only chance to find the answer to the question that haunts him: how to avoid death.

Lines 61–100: Reaching the Mountains of Mashu

After many days of travel, Gilgamesh reaches the **Mountains of Mashu**, which guard the entrance to the land of the gods. These twin peaks reach into the heavens and descend into the underworld. The mountains are guarded by **scorpion-men**, terrifying beings who protect the entrance and allow no mortal to pass.

Gilgamesh stands before the scorpion-men, filled with awe and fear. The scorpion-men see him and speak to each other: "Who is this man who dares to approach the Mountains of Mashu? No mortal has ever come this far."

The scorpion-men address Gilgamesh: "Why have you come here, Gilgamesh? This is the land of the gods, and no mortal may pass. Turn back, for this journey is not for the living."

Lines 101–140: Gilgamesh's Plea to the Scorpion-Men

Gilgamesh pleads with the scorpion-men, explaining his purpose: "I am Gilgamesh, king of Uruk. I have come in search of Utnapishtim, the one who was granted eternal life by the gods. My friend Enkidu has died, and I am filled with fear of death. I seek the secret of immortality so that I may not meet the same fate."

The scorpion-men are moved by Gilgamesh's determination and recognize his divine heritage, as he is two-thirds god and one-third man. They speak to him with compassion: "Gilgamesh, your journey is long and dangerous, and the path ahead leads into darkness. No mortal has ever traveled the road that you now seek to take. The way through the Mountains of Mashu is the way of the sun god, **Shamash**. It is a journey of twelve leagues through complete darkness, where no light shines."

Despite the dangers, Gilgamesh remains resolute. "I will go," he says. "I fear death more than the darkness. I must find Utnapishtim and learn the secret of eternal life."

Seeing Gilgamesh's resolve, the scorpion-men allow him to pass through the gates of the Mountains of Mashu.

Lines 141–180: The Passage Through Darkness

Gilgamesh enters the tunnel that runs through the Mountains of Mashu. It is the path that the sun god Shamash takes each night as he travels beneath the earth before rising again in the morning. The tunnel is long, stretching twelve leagues, and is filled with absolute darkness. There is no light, no sound, and no sense of time.

As he journeys through the tunnel, Gilgamesh feels the weight of the darkness pressing down on him. He moves quickly, driven by fear and desperation, as he knows that if he does not reach the other side before dawn, he will be trapped in the darkness forever.

For one league, he walks in darkness. Then two leagues, then three. The darkness surrounds him, and he cannot see his own hand before his face.

After six leagues, Gilgamesh grows tired, but he presses on. He knows that turning back is not an option. He must continue forward.

Finally, after twelve leagues, Gilgamesh emerges from the tunnel into the light. He has reached the end of the path, and before him lies the beautiful **Garden of the Gods**.

Lines 181–210: The Garden of the Gods

Gilgamesh finds himself in a magnificent garden, unlike anything he has ever seen. The trees are covered in jewels—lapis lazuli, carnelian, and pearls—and the fruits that grow from the branches are radiant with the colors of precious stones. The air is filled with the scent of the gods, and the ground is covered in lush green grass.

He marvels at the sight before him, but he knows that his journey is not yet over. He must continue onward to find Utnapishtim, who lives far beyond the Garden of the Gods, across the Waters of Death.

As Gilgamesh walks through the garden, he meets **Siduri**, the divine tavern-keeper who dwells at the edge of the world. She watches over the entrance to the Waters of Death and offers hospitality to those who seek the farthest shores.

Lines 211–240: Meeting Siduri, the Tavern-Keeper

Siduri sees Gilgamesh approaching and speaks to herself: "Who is this man who walks alone through the Garden of the Gods? His face is worn with grief, and his body is weary from travel. He looks like one who has traveled far and suffered greatly."

Siduri approaches Gilgamesh and asks: "Why are you here, Gilgamesh? You are mortal, and this is the land of the gods. No mortal may cross the Waters of Death."

Gilgamesh tells her of his quest: "I seek Utnapishtim, the one who was granted eternal life by the gods. I have traveled far to find him, for I fear death and wish to escape its grasp."

Siduri, seeing the sorrow in Gilgamesh's heart, advises him to abandon his quest. "Gilgamesh, no one can escape death. The gods reserved immortality for themselves, and they gave death to mankind. You will not find what you seek."

She continues, "Enjoy your life, Gilgamesh. Cherish the days you have. Eat, drink, and be merry. Spend time with your family and loved ones, for that is the lot of man. Do not chase after what the gods have kept for themselves."

Lines 241–270: Gilgamesh's Determination

Despite Siduri's words, Gilgamesh remains determined to continue his journey. He refuses to accept that death is inevitable and insists on crossing the Waters of Death to reach Utnapishtim.

Siduri, seeing that Gilgamesh will not be swayed, tells him: "If you wish to cross the Waters of Death, you must seek out **Urshanabi**, the ferryman of Utnapishtim. He will take you across, but be warned: the journey is perilous, and no mortal has ever made it."

Gilgamesh thanks Siduri for her advice and sets out to find Urshanabi, determined to continue his quest for immortality.

Key Themes and Analysis:

1. **Fear of Mortality**: Gilgamesh's overwhelming fear of death drives his quest to find Utnapishtim. This tablet reveals Gilgamesh's vulnerability as he grapples with the inevitability of mortality. The death of Enkidu serves as the catalyst for this fear, as Gilgamesh begins to realize that even the greatest heroes cannot escape death.
2. **The Journey as a Rite of Passage**: The journey through the Mountains of Mashu and the tunnel of darkness symbolizes a transformative experience for Gilgamesh. It is both a physical and spiritual journey, as he moves closer to confronting the reality of life and death. Emerging from the darkness into the Garden of the Gods suggests that Gilgamesh is entering a new realm of understanding.
3. **Divine Intervention and Boundaries**: The scorpion-men and Siduri represent divine figures who guide Gilgamesh on his journey, but they also caution him about the limits of mortal existence. Siduri's advice to Gilgamesh, urging him to accept death and enjoy life, reflects a fundamental theme of the epic: that mortality is a defining aspect of the human condition.
4. **The Desire for Immortality**: Gilgamesh's quest for immortality is central to the tablet. Despite warnings from both mortals and gods, he remains determined to find Utnapishtim and learn the secret of eternal life. His refusal to accept the inevitability of death underscores his desperation and highlights the universal human desire to overcome mortality.
5. **The Garden of the Gods as a Symbol of Immortality**: The Garden of the Gods, with its jeweled trees and divine beauty, represents the unattainable paradise of the gods. It is a stark contrast to the mortal world, where death and decay

are inevitable. The garden symbolizes the divine realm that is beyond the reach of mortals, further emphasizing the separation between gods and humans.

This translation of **Tablet IX** highlights Gilgamesh's emotional and physical journey as he seeks immortality, following the death of Enkidu. His encounters with the scorpion-men, Siduri, and the Garden of the Gods deepen the themes of mortality, human limitation, and the quest for meaning in life. The tablet sets the stage for Gilgamesh's continued journey, where he will eventually meet Utnapishtim and confront the reality of life and death.

Tablet X of the *Epic of Gilgamesh*, titled "Gilgamesh Meets Utnapishtim," continues Gilgamesh's quest for immortality. After leaving the Garden of the Gods, Gilgamesh seeks out **Urshanabi**, the ferryman who can take him across the Waters of Death to meet **Utnapishtim**, the immortal man who survived the Great Flood. In this tablet, Gilgamesh reflects on his fear of death and his grief over Enkidu, and he eventually reaches Utnapishtim, who begins to tell him the story of his own journey to immortality.

Here is a translation of **Tablet X: Gilgamesh Meets Utnapishtim**:

Tablet X: Gilgamesh Meets Utnapishtim

Lines 1–30: Gilgamesh Seeks Urshanabi

After receiving advice from Siduri, the divine tavern-keeper, Gilgamesh sets out to find **Urshanabi**, the ferryman of Utnapishtim, who alone can take him across the Waters of Death. Gilgamesh reaches the place where Urshanabi tends to his boat, a place guarded by **stone charms**, magical objects that protect the boat from the dangerous waters.

Gilgamesh, in his frustration and grief, attacks and destroys the stone charms, unaware of their purpose. Urshanabi sees this and confronts Gilgamesh, demanding to know why he has come.

"Who are you, who dares to destroy the stone charms? These are sacred, and they protect us from the deadly waters. Without them, how can you hope to cross the Waters of Death?"

Lines 31–60: Gilgamesh Explains His Quest

Gilgamesh, realizing his mistake, explains his journey and his desperate search for immortality. He tells Urshanabi of the death of his friend Enkidu and the fear of death that now haunts him.

"I am Gilgamesh, king of Uruk. My friend Enkidu has died, and I am consumed by grief. I fear that death will come for me as well, as it does for all men. That is why I seek Utnapishtim, the one who was granted eternal life by the gods. I must learn the secret of immortality."

Urshanabi listens to Gilgamesh's plea and feels sympathy for him. He understands the pain that Gilgamesh is going through but tells him that immortality is not easily gained.

"You have traveled far, Gilgamesh, and you have faced many hardships. But the journey across the Waters of Death is perilous, and now that the stone charms are destroyed, we will need to find another way to cross."

Lines 61–100: Preparing for the Journey

Urshanabi instructs Gilgamesh to go into the forest and cut down 120 poles, each 60 cubits long. These poles will be used to push the boat across the Waters of Death, since the stone charms that protected the boat from the deadly waters are now gone.

Gilgamesh, though exhausted from his long journey, immediately sets to work. He cuts down the poles and returns to Urshanabi. Together, they prepare the boat for the crossing.

Lines 101–140: Crossing the Waters of Death

With the boat ready, Gilgamesh and Urshanabi begin their journey across the Waters of Death. The waters are treacherous, and contact with them is fatal. Urshanabi warns Gilgamesh to be cautious as they cross.

Using the poles, Gilgamesh pushes the boat forward, careful not to touch the water. He uses up one pole, then another, as they slowly make their way across the dangerous waters. After using up all 120 poles, Gilgamesh removes his clothing and holds it up like a sail to catch the wind and propel them forward.

At last, they reach the far shore, the land where **Utnapishtim**, the Faraway, lives.

Lines 141–170: Gilgamesh Meets Utnapishtim

When they arrive, Gilgamesh sees Utnapishtim from afar. Utnapishtim looks like any ordinary man, not the godlike figure Gilgamesh had imagined. Surprised by his appearance, Gilgamesh approaches Utnapishtim and speaks to him.

"You are Utnapishtim, the one who was granted eternal life by the gods? You look no different from any other man.

Tablet XI of the *Epic of Gilgamesh*, also known as "The Story of the Flood and Gilgamesh's Return," contains one of the most famous sections of the epic, recounting a flood myth that bears striking similarities to the story of Noah's Ark from the Bible. In this tablet, **Utnapishtim** tells Gilgamesh the story of how he was granted immortality by the gods after surviving a great flood. Gilgamesh, seeking eternal life, listens intently, but he soon learns that immortality is beyond his reach. However, Utnapishtim offers him advice and a special plant that can restore youth. Despite this opportunity, fate intervenes, and Gilgamesh must face the reality of his mortality.

Here is a translation of **Tablet XI: The Story of the Flood and Gilgamesh's Return**:

Tablet XI: The Story of the Flood and Gilgamesh's Return

Lines 1–30: Gilgamesh Meets Utnapishtim

Gilgamesh has finally reached **Utnapishtim**, the one who was granted eternal life by the gods. He is eager to learn the secret of immortality. Utnapishtim, seeing the weariness and grief in Gilgamesh, speaks to him:

"There is no permanence in life, Gilgamesh. The gods gave death to mankind and kept immortality for themselves. Why do you seek something that is not meant for you?"

Gilgamesh responds, "I have journeyed far, through great dangers, to find you. I am afraid of death. My friend Enkidu has died, and I cannot bear the thought that I, too, will one day die. I must know how you came to possess eternal life."

Lines 31–60: Utnapishtim Begins the Flood Story

Utnapishtim listens to Gilgamesh's plea and begins to recount the story of the great flood, which led to his immortality. He says:

"I will tell you a secret of the gods, something that no man has heard before. Long ago, in the city of **Shuruppak**, which lies on the banks of the Euphrates, the gods decided to destroy mankind with a flood. The gods were angry with humanity, and they met in council to plan the flood."

Lines 61–90: The Decision to Destroy Humanity

The great gods, **Anu**, **Enlil**, **Ninurta**, **Ennuge**, and **Ea**, held a secret council and agreed to bring a flood to wipe out humanity. But the god **Ea**, who cared for mankind, warned me, Utnapishtim, of the coming disaster.

Ea whispered to me in a dream, saying, 'Man of Shuruppak, tear down your house and build a boat. Abandon your possessions and save your life. Take with you the seed of all living things, and be ready for the flood that will cover the earth.'

Lines 91–120: Utnapishtim Builds the Boat

I followed Ea's command. I built a boat, as he instructed, making it strong and watertight. The boat was six stories high, with a roof and sides as secure as the vault of the heavens. I gathered my family and animals of every kind—wild beasts, domesticated animals, and all creatures that walk the earth.

When the boat was ready, the rains began to fall. The storm gods unleashed their fury, and the floodwaters rose. For seven days and seven nights, the flood swept over the earth, destroying everything in its path. Mankind was drowned, and the land was submerged beneath the waters.

Lines 121–150: The Flood Recedes

On the seventh day, the storm subsided, and the floodwaters began to recede. I looked out of the boat and saw that the world was covered in water. After many days, the boat came to rest on the **Mountains of Nimush**. I released a dove to see if the waters had receded, but it returned, finding no resting place.

I then released a swallow, but it too returned. Finally, I released a raven, which did not return, indicating that the waters had receded enough for dry land to appear.

Lines 151–180: Utnapishtim and His Family Are Granted Immortality

When I saw that the earth was dry, I made an offering to the gods, burning incense and sacrificing animals. The gods smelled the sweet fragrance and gathered around the offering. But **Enlil**, who had decreed the flood, was enraged that anyone had survived.

The god **Ea** spoke to Enlil, saying, 'Why did you bring this flood upon humanity? Could you not have punished them with a lesser disaster? Now, because of you, mankind is nearly destroyed.'

Enlil's anger subsided, and he approached me and my wife. He touched our foreheads and said, 'You and your wife shall live forever. The gods have granted you immortality. You will dwell far away, at the mouth of the rivers, beyond the reach of mortals.'

That is how I, Utnapishtim, came to live forever. But, Gilgamesh, this gift is not meant for you. The gods reserved immortality for themselves, and they gave death to all mortals.

Lines 181–210: The Test of Staying Awake

Gilgamesh is disheartened to hear that immortality is beyond his grasp. Utnapishtim, feeling pity for him, offers him a test: "If you wish to gain immortality, prove your worth. Stay awake for six days and seven nights. If you can do this, the gods may grant you eternal life."

Gilgamesh, exhausted from his long journey, sits down to take the test, but almost immediately, he falls asleep.

Utnapishtim's wife bakes a loaf of bread each day, placing one beside Gilgamesh to mark the passage of time.

On the seventh day, Utnapishtim wakes Gilgamesh and shows him the loaves of bread, now hardened with age. "You have failed the test, Gilgamesh. You could not stay awake. How can you hope to conquer death when you cannot conquer sleep?"

Lines 211–250: The Plant of Youth

Despairing, Gilgamesh prepares to leave. Utnapishtim, feeling sympathy for him, offers him a consolation: "There is a plant that grows at the bottom of the sea. It is called the **Plant of Heartbeat**. It can restore youth to anyone who eats it. Though you cannot gain immortality, you may take this plant and use it to restore your youth."

With Urshanabi's help, Gilgamesh ties stones to his feet and descends to the bottom of the sea, where he finds the plant. Triumphant, he returns to the shore and plans to take the plant back to Uruk. He hopes to share it with the elders of his city and rejuvenate them as well.

Lines 251–280: The Snake Steals the Plant

On the journey back to Uruk, Gilgamesh stops to rest by a pool of water. As he bathes, a serpent comes and steals the plant. The serpent eats the plant and immediately sheds its skin, symbolizing the renewal of youth.

Gilgamesh sees the plant is gone and weeps. "I have failed," he says. "The one thing that could restore my youth is gone. I will never escape death."

Lines 281–320: Gilgamesh Returns to Uruk

With a heavy heart, Gilgamesh returns to Uruk, empty-handed and accepting the reality of his mortality. As he approaches the city, he reflects on his journey and on the great walls of Uruk that he had built.

He speaks to Urshanabi: "Look at the walls of Uruk, the great city. They will stand for generations, long after I am gone. Though I cannot live forever, my deeds and my city will endure. This is my legacy."

Key Themes and Analysis:

1. **The Flood Myth**: The story of the flood in **Tablet XI** is one of the most famous parts of the *Epic of Gilgamesh*. The similarities to the story of Noah's Ark in the Bible are striking, and this flood myth is one of the earliest recorded in human history. Utnapishtim's survival of the flood and the granting of immortality to him and his wife show the deep interplay between divine wrath and mercy in Mesopotamian myth.
2. **The Limits of Mortality**: Utnapishtim's story reinforces the theme that immortality is reserved for the gods, and death is an inevitable part of the human condition. Gilgamesh's quest for eternal life ends in disappointment, as he learns that immortality is not something that can be achieved by human effort.
3. **The Test of Staying Awake**: Utnapishtim's challenge to Gilgamesh to stay awake for six days and seven nights is symbolic of the impossible nature of his quest. Sleep, like death, is an inescapable part of human life. By failing the test,

Gilgamesh is forced to confront his limitations as a mortal.
4. **The Plant of Youth**: The plant that can restore youth offers a glimmer of hope to Gilgamesh, but this hope is quickly dashed when the snake steals the plant. The snake's shedding of its skin symbolizes the renewal of life, but this renewal is reserved for the serpent, not for Gilgamesh. This reinforces the idea that humans cannot escape death.
5. **Legacy Over Immortality**: In the end, Gilgamesh realizes that while he

Tablet XII of the *Epic of Gilgamesh*, often regarded as an appendix or later addition to the epic, differs in tone and theme from the preceding eleven tablets. It appears to be a separate Sumerian narrative, focusing on the spirit of **Enkidu** and his journey to the underworld. This tablet doesn't directly continue the narrative of Gilgamesh's quest for immortality but instead delves into Mesopotamian views on the afterlife, the underworld, and the rituals associated with death.

Here is a translation of **Tablet XII: Enkidu's Spirit and the Underworld**:

Tablet XII: Enkidu's Spirit and the Underworld

Lines 1–30: The Sacred Objects and the Journey Begins

Gilgamesh, still mourning the death of his friend **Enkidu**, desires to recover certain sacred objects—his **pukku** (drum) and **mikku** (drumstick)—which have fallen into the underworld. These objects symbolize power and connection to the divine. He speaks to Enkidu, asking for his help in retrieving them from the underworld.

Gilgamesh says to Enkidu: "My drum and drumstick have fallen into the underworld, and I cannot reach them. You, my brother, must go down into the underworld and retrieve them for me."

Enkidu agrees to help and prepares to descend into the underworld. But before he goes, Gilgamesh gives him strict instructions on how to behave in the realm of the dead.

Lines 31–60: Gilgamesh's Instructions to Enkidu

Gilgamesh warns Enkidu about the strict rules of the underworld and advises him to take great care not to violate any of them. He says:

"Enkidu, if you must enter the underworld, heed my words:

- Do not wear clean clothes, for the dead will think you are rich.
- Do not anoint yourself with fine oil, for the dead will surround you.
- Do not carry a staff, for the spirits will see it as a threat.
- Do not wear sandals, for they will draw attention to you.

- Do not kiss your wife or strike your wife, for it will offend the spirits of the dead.
- Do not shout or make noise in the underworld, for it is a silent realm."

Despite Gilgamesh's warnings, Enkidu forgets or disregards these instructions and enters the underworld improperly dressed and behaving in a way that angers the spirits.

Lines 61–90: Enkidu Trapped in the Underworld

Enkidu descends into the underworld to retrieve the drum and drumstick, but because he violated the rules of the underworld, he is trapped there. The shades of the dead surround him, and he is no longer able to return to the land of the living.

Gilgamesh, realizing that Enkidu has not returned, becomes worried. He prays to the gods for help, hoping to learn the fate of his friend.

Lines 91–120: Gilgamesh Prays to the Gods

Gilgamesh offers prayers to the gods, seeking aid in recovering Enkidu from the underworld. He first appeals to the god **Enlil**, but Enlil refuses to intervene. Gilgamesh then turns to the moon god **Sin**, but Sin also declines to help.

Finally, Gilgamesh prays to the god of wisdom, **Ea**, and to **Shamash**, the sun god, who can travel between the worlds of the living and the dead. Shamash, taking pity on Gilgamesh, agrees to help and opens a crack in the earth, allowing Enkidu's spirit to rise from the underworld.

Lines 121–150: The Return of Enkidu's Spirit

Enkidu's spirit emerges from the underworld and speaks to Gilgamesh. Gilgamesh, relieved to see his friend again, eagerly asks Enkidu about the conditions of the underworld and what fate awaits the dead.

Gilgamesh says: "Tell me, my friend, what is it like in the underworld? What have you seen there?"

Enkidu responds with sorrow and dread, describing the bleak and joyless existence of the dead.

Lines 151–180: Enkidu Describes the Underworld

Enkidu begins to describe the underworld, painting a grim picture of the afterlife:

"The underworld is a place of darkness and dust. The dead eat clay and drink dirt. They are clothed like birds, in feathers, and they live in darkness, never seeing the light of the sun.

Those who had many sons are honored in death, while those who had no children are forgotten. The dead who were respected in life have some comfort, but those who were neglected or who died in shame are tormented. The fate of each soul is determined by how they lived and how they were remembered by the living."

Gilgamesh listens in silence, filled with sadness at the hopelessness of the underworld.

Lines 181–210: Specific Fates of the Dead

Enkidu continues, describing the specific fates of various individuals:

"The man who has left behind many sons is at peace, for his sons pour libations in his honor. But the man who died without children sits alone in the underworld, without anyone to remember him.

The man who died in battle is honored and rests well, but the man who drowned in the river is forgotten and wanders without rest.

The man whose body lies unburied on the battlefield has no peace. He roams the earth without a home, for his spirit cannot find rest until his body is properly buried."

Lines 211–240: The End of the Story

Gilgamesh is deeply affected by Enkidu's words. The descriptions of the afterlife reinforce the inevitability of death and the importance of legacy and remembrance. Gilgamesh now fully understands the futility of seeking immortality and realizes that one's actions and how they are remembered are what truly matter.

The tablet concludes with Gilgamesh pondering the fate of all mortals and the sadness of life's impermanence, as he returns to Uruk to continue his reign, now more aware of the finality of death.

Key Themes and Analysis:

1. **The Bleakness of the Afterlife**: Tablet XII provides a detailed vision of the Mesopotamian

underworld, which is portrayed as a place of darkness, dust, and despair. The dead are cut off from the joys of life, and even the most honored souls live in a dreary existence. This depiction of the underworld emphasizes the importance of life on earth and the finality of death.
2. **The Role of Legacy**: Enkidu's description of the different fates of the dead highlights the importance of legacy and remembrance. Those who are remembered and honored by the living can find some peace in death, while those who are forgotten or neglected suffer eternally. This underscores the idea that immortality, in a sense, comes through the memory of others and how one is honored after death.
3. **Gilgamesh's Acceptance of Mortality**: The tablet, while somewhat disconnected from the main narrative, reinforces the theme of mortality that permeates the epic. By speaking with Enkidu's spirit, Gilgamesh is once again confronted with the inevitability of death, not only for himself but for all mortals. He begins to understand that immortality is unattainable and that he must focus on living a life that will be remembered.
4. **Ritual and the Afterlife**: The importance of burial rites and the actions of the living toward the dead are crucial themes in this tablet. Those who are honored with proper burials and libations are able to rest in the underworld, while those whose bodies are left unburied are doomed to wander the earth. This reflects the significance of funerary rituals in Mesopotamian culture and their belief in the continued relationship between the living and the dead.
5. **Separation from the Main Narrative**: Scholars often view **Tablet XII** as a later addition to the

epic, as its style and content diverge from the main story of Gilgamesh's quest for immortality. While the previous tablet, **Tablet XI**, provides a conclusion to Gilgamesh's journey and his realization that immortality is impossible, Tablet XII shifts the focus back to Enkidu's spirit and the underworld. This has led to the belief that Tablet XII may be based on earlier Sumerian stories about Gilgamesh and Enkidu, such as *The Death of Bilgames*.

This translation of **Tablet XII** provides a glimpse into Mesopotamian beliefs about the afterlife and the fate of the dead. Though it feels somewhat disconnected from the main narrative arc of the *Epic of Gilgamesh*, it reinforces key themes of mortality, legacy, and the importance of remembrance. Through his interactions with Enkidu's spirit, Gilgamesh comes to a deeper understanding of the finality of death and the meaning of life.

The Code of Ur-Nammu

The *Code of Ur-Nammu*, dating to around 2100–2050 BCE, is one of the earliest surviving legal codes. It was written during the reign of King Ur-Nammu of Ur, a Sumerian city-state, and is notable for laying the groundwork for later legal systems, including the famous *Code of Hammurabi*. Although the *Code of Ur-Nammu* is fragmentary, scholars have reconstructed many of its laws based on various discovered tablets. The laws are primarily written in Sumerian and are known for using fines as penalties, rather than physical punishment.

Here are the surviving sections of the *Code of Ur-Nammu*, with the laws that have been reconstructed:

Prologue (Surviving Fragment)

The prologue introduces King **Ur-Nammu** as the chosen ruler by the gods, especially the moon god **Nanna**. The king boasts of bringing justice and peace to the land, protecting the weak, and ensuring fairness. Ur-Nammu claims divine authority to issue the laws that follow, stating that his rule is intended to ensure justice and order in society.

Laws of the Code of Ur-Nammu

1. **If a man commits murder, that man must be killed.**

- Capital punishment is prescribed for the crime of murder, reflecting the seriousness of taking a life.
2. **If a man commits robbery, he is to be killed.**
    - Similar to murder, robbery is treated as a capital offense under this law.
3. **If a man commits kidnapping, he is to be imprisoned and pay 15 shekels of silver.**
    - Unlike murder and robbery, kidnapping results in imprisonment and a fine rather than death.
4. **If a slave marries a free person, he/she is to hand over the firstborn son to his master.**
    - This law regulates marriage between slaves and free persons, specifying that the firstborn child must be given to the slave's owner.
5. **If a man causes the loss of another man's eye, he must pay half a mina (approximately 250 grams) of silver.**
    - Compensation for physical harm (the loss of an eye) is prescribed, with a set amount of silver to be paid to the injured party.
6. **If a man breaks another man's bone, he must pay one mina of silver.**
    - Another form of compensation for bodily harm, where a fine is imposed for breaking a bone.
7. **If a man cuts off another man's foot, he must pay ten shekels of silver.**
    - A specific penalty is set for the loss of a foot, with the compensation being lower than for breaking a bone but still significant.
8. **If a man divorces his first wife, he must pay her one mina of silver.**

- This law provides for compensation for a wife in the case of divorce, ensuring some protection for the woman.

9. **If a man divorces his second wife, he must pay her one mina of silver.**
   - The same compensation applies to a second wife, reflecting the importance of maintaining justice in marriage and divorce.

10. **If a man falsely accuses someone of a crime, he must pay 10 shekels of silver.**
    - A fine is imposed on anyone who makes a false accusation, discouraging slander and wrongful accusations.

11. **If a man's slave-girl commits a crime and is found guilty, the owner must pay 10 shekels of silver.**
    - The slave-owner is responsible for the actions of their slave, and a fine is imposed on the owner if the slave-girl commits a crime.

12. **If a man knocks out the tooth of another man, he shall pay two shekels of silver.**
    - Compensation is required for less severe injuries, such as the loss of a tooth.

13. **If a slave says to his master, "You are not my master," his ear shall be cut off.**
    - This law imposes physical punishment for slaves who openly rebel against their masters.

Summary of the Legal System

The *Code of Ur-Nammu* is significant for establishing an early form of law that emphasizes restitution over retribution. Many of the penalties involve fines paid in silver, rather than the "eye for an eye" type of justice that would later become more prevalent in the *Code of Hammurabi*. The code demonstrates a concern for social order, fairness, and the protection of various classes of people, including slaves and women.

Epilogue (Surviving Fragment)

The epilogue, like the prologue, praises King Ur-Nammu as a just and wise ruler, blessed by the gods to establish laws that would bring order and prosperity to his people. It highlights his accomplishments and the peace that his legal system brought to Sumer.

Conclusion

The *Code of Ur-Nammu* is a foundational legal document that provides insight into the early legal practices of Mesopotamian society. It emphasizes compensation and fines for most crimes, with a few cases (like murder and robbery) warranting the death penalty. This early legal system reflects the values of justice, protection of property, and maintaining social harmony. Although many sections of the code remain lost, what survives shows that the Sumerians developed one of the most advanced legal systems of their time.

The Code of Ur-Nammu

- **Found**: The *Code of Ur-Nammu* was discovered in the ancient city of Nippur (modern-day Iraq) during excavations by the University of Pennsylvania.
- **Currently housed**:
    - The tablets are part of the collection at the **University of Pennsylvania Museum of Archaeology and Anthropology**, Philadelphia.
    - Other fragments of this code are held at the **Istanbul Archaeological Museums**, Turkey.

The Sumerian King List

The *Sumerian King List* is an ancient manuscript originally written in the Sumerian language, providing a chronological record of kings from various city-states in ancient Sumer (southern Mesopotamia). It lists the kings, the lengths of their reigns, and often includes divine or semi-mythical figures who ruled before the historical period. It starts with the kings who reigned before the flood and extends into more historically verifiable periods. While the list is not entirely historical (some reigns are impossibly long and some kings are mythical), it gives valuable insights into how the Sumerians understood their history.

Here is the **complete Sumerian King List** as reconstructed from multiple surviving copies of the text:

- **Found**: The *Sumerian King List* was discovered in various locations, including Nippur and Larsa (modern-day Iraq), in multiple copies. The most famous copy was found in the city of Nippur.
- **Currently housed**:
    - One of the best-preserved copies is housed in the **Ashmolean Museum**, Oxford, UK.
    - Other fragments are kept at the **Iraq Museum**, Baghdad, and **Penn Museum**, Philadelphia.

Antediluvian (Before the Flood) Kings

1. **Alulim** of Eridu:
   Reigned 28,800 years.
   "After the kingship descended from heaven, the kingship was in Eridu."
2. **Alalngar** of Eridu:
   Reigned 36,000 years.
3. **Enmenluanna** of Bad-tibira:
   Reigned 43,200 years.
   "In Bad-tibira, Enmenluanna became king."
4. **Enmengalanna** of Bad-tibira:
   Reigned 28,800 years.
5. **Dumuzid the Shepherd** of Bad-tibira:
   Reigned 36,000 years.
6. **Enmenunna** of Larak:
   Reigned 43,200 years.
   "In Larak, Enmenunna became king."
7. **Ensipadzidana** of Larak:
   Reigned 28,800 years.
8. **Enmenduranna** of Sippar:
   Reigned 21,000 years.
9. **Ubara-Tutu** of Shuruppak:
   Reigned 18,600 years.
   "In Shuruppak, Ubara-Tutu became king."
10. **Ziusudra** (Ziusudra of Shuruppak) — (The hero of the Sumerian Flood story).

After the flood had swept over, the kingship again descended from heaven.

Postdiluvian (After the Flood) Kings

First Dynasty of Kish

1. **Jushur** of Kish:
   Reigned 1,200 years.
2. **Kullassina-bel** of Kish:
   Reigned 960 years.
   (The name Kullassina-bel means "All of them were lord.")
3. **Nangishlishma** of Kish:
   Reigned 670 years.
4. **En-tarah-ana** of Kish:
   Reigned 420 years.
5. **Babum** of Kish:
   Reigned 300 years.
6. **Puannum** of Kish:
   Reigned 840 years.
7. **Kalibum** of Kish:
   Reigned 960 years.
8. **Kalumum** of Kish:
   Reigned 840 years.
9. **Zuqaqip** of Kish:
   Reigned 900 years.
10. **Atab** of Kish:
    Reigned 600 years.
11. **Mashda** of Kish:
    Reigned 840 years.
12. **Arwium** of Kish:
    Reigned 720 years.
13. **Etana** of Kish:
    Reigned 1,500 years.
    (Etana is a legendary king, said to have "ascended to heaven and consolidated all the lands.")
14. **Balih** of Kish:
    Reigned 400 years.
15. **En-me-nuna** of Kish:
    Reigned 660 years.
16. **Melem-Kish** of Kish:
    Reigned 900 years.

17. **Barsal-nuna** of Kish:
    Reigned 1,200 years.
18. **Zamug** of Kish:
    Reigned 140 years.
19. **Tizqar** of Kish:
    Reigned 305 years.
20. **Ilku** of Kish:
    Reigned 900 years.
21. **Iltasadum** of Kish:
    Reigned 1,200 years.
22. **En-me-baragesi** of Kish:
    Reigned 900 years.
    (Historically attested; his name appears on inscriptions.)
23. **Aga of Kish**:
    Reigned 625 years.
    (Aga is the son of En-me-baragesi and is also attested in the *Epic of Gilgamesh*.)

First Dynasty of Uruk

1. **Meskiagkasher** of Uruk:
   Reigned 324 years.
   (Said to be the son of the sun god Utu.)
2. **Enmerkar** of Uruk:
   Reigned 420 years.
   (A legendary king, subject of the *Enmerkar and the Lord of Aratta* epic.)
3. **Lugalbanda** of Uruk:
   Reigned 1,200 years.
   (Lugalbanda is a mythical king and is a central character in Sumerian poetry.)
4. **Dumuzid the Fisherman** of Uruk:
   Reigned 100 years.

5. **Gilgamesh** of Uruk:
   Reigned 126 years.
   (Gilgamesh is the hero of the *Epic of Gilgamesh* and a central figure in Sumerian and Akkadian mythology.)
6. **Ur-Nungal** of Uruk:
   Reigned 30 years.
7. **Udul-Kalama** of Uruk:
   Reigned 15 years.
8. **La-ba'shum** of Uruk:
   Reigned 9 years.
9. **En-nun-tarah-ana** of Uruk:
   Reigned 8 years.
10. **Mesh-He** of Uruk:
    Reigned 36 years.

First Dynasty of Ur

1. **Mesh-Ane-pada** of Ur:
   Reigned 80 years.
2. **Mesh-Kiag-Nuna** of Ur:
   Reigned 36 years.
3. **Elulu** of Ur:
   Reigned 25 years.
4. **Balulu** of Ur:
   Reigned 36 years.

Second Dynasty of Kish

1. **Susuda** of Kish:
   Reigned 201 years.

2. **Dadasig** of Kish:
   Reigned 81 years.
3. **Mamagal** of Kish:
   Reigned 360 years.
4. **Kalbum** of Kish:
   Reigned 195 years.
5. **Tuge** of Kish:
   Reigned 360 years.
6. **Men-nuna** of Kish:
   Reigned 180 years.

Dynasty of Awan

1. **Puzur-Nirah** of Awan:
   Reigned 420 years.
2. **Ku-ulmu** of Awan:
   Reigned 960 years.
3. **Naram-Sin** of Awan:
   Reigned 1,200 years.

Third Dynasty of Kish

1. **Kubaba** of Kish:
   Reigned 100 years.
   (Kubaba is notable as the only woman on the Sumerian King List and was later deified.)

Conclusion of the Sumerian King List

The *Sumerian King List* concludes with several other dynasties, including those of **Akshak**, **Mari**, and **Agade**, and continues into historical kings whose reigns are more likely to have been recorded accurately. The list emphasizes the divine origin of kingship, showing how kingship was passed from city to city according to the will of the gods. It blends myth and history, with some reigns being impossibly long and others more grounded in reality, such as Gilgamesh and En-me-baragesi, who are both attested in historical records outside of the list.

Historical and Mythological Significance

The *Sumerian King List* provides a fascinating glimpse into the early Sumerian worldview, blending myth, religion, and historical record. It demonstrates how the Sumerians believed that kingship was divinely ordained and cyclical, moving from one city to another. Although much of the list is mythological or exaggerated, the later portions provide valuable insights into real historical figures and the political structure of ancient Mesopotamia.

The Temple Hymns of Enheduanna

The **Sumerian Temple Hymns** and other religious texts are among the earliest forms of recorded poetry and prayers in human history. These hymns were composed to honor the gods, temples, and cities of Sumer, and they reflect the Sumerians' religious beliefs, rituals, and cosmology. The temple hymns, attributed to the Sumerian priestess and poet **Enheduanna**, daughter of King Sargon of Akkad, are particularly important. Enheduanna is one of the earliest known authors in world history. These hymns honor various deities and temples throughout Mesopotamia.

Below is a selection of the **Sumerian Temple Hymns** and **religious texts** as they have survived. While the exact number of hymns varies, the collection typically focuses on a range of cities, their gods, and the sacred temples that were believed to house divine power.

- **Found**: These were found in the city of Lagash (modern Tell al-Hiba, Iraq) and other temple sites such as Nippur.
- **Currently housed**:
    - Tablets with hymns and inscriptions are in the **Louvre Museum**, Paris.
    - Other important fragments are in the **British Museum**, London, and **Iraq Museum**, Baghdad.

Hymn 1: The Temple of Enlil in Nippur

O House, great crown reaching heaven,

Abode of Enlil,

Your foundation is enduring;

Your doorposts, the gateway of heaven.

O temple, lofty sanctuary,

Whose shadow stretches over the land,

Your interior is the divine chamber of kingship.

Hymn 2: The Temple of Inanna in Uruk

O Eanna, splendid light,

House of the queen of heaven, Inanna,

You rise like the great mountains.

Your neck is adorned with the heavens,

Your terraces breathe with majesty.

In your shade the people find peace,

And to your shrine all hearts turn.

Hymn 3: The Temple of Nanna in Ur

O House of the Great Light,

The dwelling of Nanna,

In the holy city of Ur you stand.

Your walls rise up to heaven,

Your brilliance shines like the stars.

You shelter the moon god, father of time,

And in your courts, kings bend low.

Hymn 4: The Temple of Ninlil in Kesh

O E-kur, sacred house,

The dwelling of Ninlil,

Your doors are majestic,

Your chambers are filled with abundance.

O Kesh, your mother Ninlil abides in you,

And your fields overflow with grain.

Hymn 5: The Temple of Ninhursag in Adab

O House, Great Mountain of the Earth,

The abode of Ninhursag,

Your walls are pure like lapis lazuli.

O Adab, your queen is the mother of all lands,

Your rivers flow with her blessing,

And your fields yield bountiful harvests.

Hymn 6: The Temple of Ningirsu in Lagash

O E-ninnu, great thunderbird of Lagash,

The abode of Ningirsu,

You stretch your wings over the land,

And your strength is the might of a storm.

In your temple, the black-headed people gather,

For your power protects the city.

Hymn 7: The Temple of Nanna in Urim

O Egishnugal, House of Radiance,

Home of the moon god Nanna,

Your light shines like silver in the night sky.

Your brilliance spreads peace over the city,

And your faithful come to offer their prayers.

Hymn 8: The Temple of Enki in Eridu

O Abzu, the pure temple of Enki,

The god of wisdom and waters.

Your depths are the source of life,

Your streams flow with knowledge.

Within your holy waters, the great god dwells,

And in your chambers, he bestows wisdom on mankind.

Hymn 9: The Temple of Ninurta in Nippur

O House of the warrior god Ninurta,

You stand as a mighty fortress,

Your walls are unshakable.

O Nippur, your strength is endless,

And in your midst, the storm god rages,

Bringing justice to the lands.

Hymn 10: The Temple of Utu in Sippar

O House of the rising sun,

Abode of Utu, the sun god,

You are the eye of the world.

Your light pierces the darkness,

And in your courts, the laws of truth and justice prevail.

O Sippar, you are blessed with the favor of Utu,

Your lands prosper under his gaze.

Additional Religious Texts: Prayers and Incantations

Prayer to Inanna

For Blessings of Love and Power

O Inanna, queen of heaven and earth,

Light of the world,

Your radiance fills the sky,

Your power sweeps across the land.

Grant your servant strength and wisdom,

Lend your divine favor,

And bless the people with your love.

Incantation to Enki

For Purification and Healing

O Enki, lord of the sweet waters,

Master of life and all that grows,

Cleanse me of impurity, wash away my sins.

Let your pure streams flow over me,

And may your healing touch restore my spirit.

By your wisdom, I am made whole,

By your hand, I rise anew.

Prayer for Kingship and Justice

For a Just Reign

O Shamash, bringer of justice,

Light of truth,

May the king walk in your path,

May he judge the people fairly.

Bless his reign with wisdom,

So that the strong do not oppress the weak,

And peace reigns over the land.

Incantation to Nanna

For Guidance through the Night

O Nanna, lord of the night sky,

Light my path as I walk in darkness.

As you watch over the stars,

Watch over me,

Guide me through the shadows,

And bring me safely to the dawn.

Conclusion

The *Sumerian Temple Hymns* and other religious texts provide deep insights into the spiritual life of ancient Sumerians, reflecting their devotion to a pantheon of gods, each associated with specific natural forces, cities, and aspects of life. These hymns and prayers were recited in sacred ceremonies and in the daily worship of the temples, binding the people of Sumer to their deities and ensuring the favor of the divine in their lives.

Enheduanna's role as the poet and priestess who composed many of these hymns marks a significant moment in literary history, as she is the earliest known author whose name has been recorded. Her hymns to Inanna and other gods played a central role in solidifying the religious and political authority of her father, Sargon of Akkad, by linking the divine with royal power.

Through these hymns and texts, we glimpse the ways in which the Sumerians sought to understand their world, express their piety, and maintain a connection with the gods who they believed controlled the forces of nature and human fate. These writings, engraved on clay tablets, have survived thousands of years, serving as a testament to the enduring religious and cultural practices of ancient Mesopotamia.

The **Administrative and Economic Tablets**

from ancient Sumerian and Mesopotamian civilizations provide a wealth of information about daily life, trade, taxes, labor, and agriculture. These tablets are records of economic transactions, tax collections, labor allocations, crop yields, and other activities crucial to the functioning of the Sumerian state. Most of these tablets were written in **cuneiform** script on clay tablets, serving as a form of record-keeping that allowed rulers and officials to maintain control over their territories.

Although these records are fragmentary and many are repetitive, they offer a detailed glimpse into the bureaucratic systems of the time. Below is a reconstruction of the general content of **Administrative and Economic Tablets** from ancient Sumer, reflecting the types of transactions and records that have been found.

- **Found**: Thousands of administrative and economic tablets have been found across Sumerian cities such as Ur, Uruk, Nippur, and Lagash.
- **Currently housed**:

    - **Iraq Museum**, Baghdad.
    - **Penn Museum**, Philadelphia.
    - **Louvre Museum**, Paris.
    - **British Museum**, London.
    - **Oriental Institute of the University of Chicago**, USA.

1. Grain Ration Distribution Tablets

One of the most common types of administrative tablets deals with the distribution of rations, especially grain, to workers, priests, soldiers, and other members of society. These records document the amount of grain distributed on a daily, weekly, or monthly basis, often specifying the job role or status of the recipients.

Example:

- **"Monthly Grain Ration Record"**
    - **Date**: Year of King Shulgi, month of barley harvest.
    - **Location**: City of Ur.
    - **Scribe**: Enlil-nasir, overseer of the granary.

    Workers receiving grain:

    - **Foreman**: 1 gur of grain.
    - **Laborers**: 1 ban of grain each.
    - **Priests**: 1 ban 6 sila of grain each.
    - **Women (weaving for temple)**: 1 ban of grain.

---

2. Tax Collection Tablets

These tablets record taxes collected from farmers, merchants, and craftsmen. Taxes were often paid in the form of goods (barley, dates, sheep, etc.), and these records indicate the quantity, the payer, and the purpose of the tax (temple, palace, or other civic needs).

Example:

- **"Barley Tax Record"**
  - **Date**: Year of the festival of the god Ningirsu.
  - **Location**: City of Lagash.
  - **Scribe**: Ur-Dumuzi, tax collector.

Farmers and Tax Contributions:

  - **Ur-Nanna**: 3 gur of barley.
  - **Lugal-ensi**: 5 gur of barley.
  - **Nam-Sin**: 1 gur of barley, 2 sila of sesame oil.
  - **E-Ani**: 4 gur of barley, 5 sheep.

---

3. Inventory and Supply Tablets

These tablets provide detailed lists of supplies stored in temples or palace granaries, including the quantities of raw materials such as wool, oil, grain, and precious metals. Such records were crucial for temple and palace administrations to track their wealth and manage their resources.

Example:

- **"Inventory of Temple Goods"**
  - **Date**: Year of the great festival of Inanna.
  - **Location**: Temple of Inanna, Uruk.
  - **Scribe**: Enheduanna, high priestess.

  Items in Storage:

- o **Barley**: 50 gur in granary 1.
- o **Sheep**: 80 sheep in temple pasture.
- o **Wool**: 300 bundles.
- o **Copper tools**: 12 sickles, 5 axes, 10 knives.
- o **Gold jewelry**: 5 necklaces, 3 bracelets.
- o **Beer jars**: 10 jars of date beer for festival use.

4. Labor Assignment Tablets

Labor assignment records were essential to maintaining large-scale public works, such as the building of temples, city walls, canals, and irrigation systems. These tablets record the number of laborers assigned to specific projects, their duties, and the duration of their work.

Example:

- • **"Labor Assignment Record for Canal Construction"**
  - o **Date**: Year of the completion of the Great Canal.
  - o **Location**: City of Ur.
  - o **Scribe**: Ur-Nungal, overseer of the labor force.

Labor Assigned:

- o **Foremen**: 2 (Lugal-Marduk, Ur-Nammu).
- o **Skilled stone masons**: 10 men.
- o **Unskilled laborers**: 50 men.
- o **Duration of work**: 3 months.
- o **Rations issued**: 1 gur of barley per foreman, 2 ban of grain per laborer per month.

5. Trade and Transaction Tablets

Trade was an integral part of the Mesopotamian economy, both within the empire and with distant regions. Tablets recording trade agreements and transactions document the exchange of goods like wool, grain, copper, tin, and luxury items such as lapis lazuli. These records often detail the names of traders, the goods exchanged, and the agreed-upon terms.

Example:

- **"Trade Agreement between Ur and Dilmun"**
    - **Date**: Year of the opening of the sea route to Dilmun.
    - **Location**: City of Ur.
    - **Scribe**: Ilum-Marduk, trade scribe.

    Goods Exchanged:

    - **From Ur**: 50 bundles of wool, 20 gur of barley, 10 jars of sesame oil.
    - **From Dilmun**: 10 ingots of copper, 5 sacks of dates, 20 pieces of lapis lazuli.
    - **Conditions**: Payment in full upon delivery; wool to be sent during the next month's trade caravan.

6. Land Ownership and Allocation Tablets

These tablets record land ownership, grants of land from the king or temple, and the distribution of land among individuals or families. The allocation of agricultural land was essential for supporting the economy, and these records helped manage disputes and ensure rightful ownership.

Example:

- **"Land Grant Record"**
    - **Date**: Year of the Great Harvest of Ningirsu.
    - **Location**: City of Lagash.
    - **Scribe**: Ur-Ningirsu, temple scribe.

    Grant Details:

    - **Land granted to**: Lugal-Nanna, temple servant.
    - **Size of land**: 10 iku of fertile land.
    - **Use**: For growing barley and flax for the temple of Ningirsu.
    - **Duration of grant**: Permanent, passed down to Lugal-Nanna's descendants.

7. Agricultural Output and Harvest Tablets

Agriculture was the backbone of the Sumerian economy, and these tablets document the harvest of crops, particularly barley, wheat, and dates. They include the yield, the portion allocated to the state or temple, and the remaining portion for private use or trade.

Example:

- **"Harvest Record for the Year"**
    - **Date**: Year of the great barley harvest.

- **Location**: City of Nippur.
- **Scribe**: Ninsumun, overseer of agriculture.

Harvest Yield:

- **Total yield of barley**: 100 gur.
- **Portion allocated to temple**: 30 gur.
- **Portion allocated to the king's granary**: 20 gur.
- **Portion for farmers**: 50 gur.
- **Additional yield**: 10 gur of wheat, 5 gur of dates.

8. Loan and Debt Tablets

These tablets document loans made to individuals or businesses, often involving grain or silver. The terms of repayment, including interest, are clearly outlined, and these records could later be used to settle disputes in the courts.

Example:

- **"Grain Loan Agreement"**
    - **Date**: Year of the great feast for the god Enlil.
    - **Location**: City of Nippur.
    - **Scribe**: Ur-Gula, loan recorder.

    Loan Details:

    - **Lender**: Temple of Enlil.
    - **Borrower**: Lu-Nanna, farmer.
    - **Amount borrowed**: 5 gur of barley.

- Interest: 10% annually.
- Repayment terms: Due after the next harvest; failure to repay results in seizure of land.

9. Royal Decrees and Edicts

Kings often issued decrees to regulate labor, tax rates, or land grants. These decrees were written on tablets and sent to various cities, where local administrators would ensure compliance. Some of these decrees were preserved as records of the king's law.

Example:

- **"Royal Decree on Tax Exemption"**
    - **Date**: Year of King Shulgi's fortification of the walls of Ur.
    - **Location**: City of Ur.
    - **Scribe**: Lugal-melem, royal scribe.

Decree:

- **By the order of King Shulgi**, the people of Ur are exempt from grain taxes for one year due to the successful completion of the city walls. This decree applies to all citizens, including farmers, merchants, and artisans.

Conclusion

The **Administrative and Economic Tablets** from ancient Sumer provide a detailed account of the daily workings of an advanced civilization, illustrating how early governments managed resources, taxes, trade, and labor. These tablets are invaluable sources of information about Sumerian life, offering insights into everything from agricultural practices to royal edicts. Preserved for thousands of years, these clay tablets continue to shed light on the sophisticated bureaucratic systems that supported the world's first urbanized societies.

The Inscriptions on Monuments and Steles

from ancient Mesopotamia were important vehicles for proclaiming the deeds of kings, military victories, religious dedications, and territorial claims. These inscriptions were typically carved into large stone slabs (steles) or monuments and served as public declarations of the power, legitimacy, and divine favor of rulers. Some of the most famous inscriptions, like the **Stele of Hammurabi** and the **Victory Stele of Naram-Sin**, have survived, offering valuable historical insight into the politics, warfare, and religious beliefs of the time.

Below are reconstructions of several significant **Inscriptions on Monuments and Steles** from Sumer, Akkad, and Babylon:

The **Inscriptions on Monuments and Steles** from ancient Mesopotamia were important vehicles for proclaiming the deeds of kings, military victories, religious dedications, and territorial claims. These inscriptions were typically carved into large stone slabs (steles) or monuments and served as public declarations of the power, legitimacy, and divine favor of rulers. Some of the most famous inscriptions, like the **Stele of Hammurabi** and the **Victory Stele of Naram-Sin**, have survived, offering valuable historical insight into the politics, warfare, and religious beliefs of the time.

Below are reconstructions of several significant **Inscriptions on Monuments and Steles** from Sumer, Akkad, and Babylon:

- **Found**: The Stele of the Vultures, which commemorates the victory of King Eannatum of Lagash, was discovered in Telloh (ancient Girsu), near Lagash (modern-day Iraq).
- **Currently housed**:

  - The stele is housed in the **Louvre Museum**, Paris.

1. The Stele of Hammurabi (Circa 1754 BCE)

Context: The Stele of Hammurabi is one of the most famous legal inscriptions from ancient Mesopotamia. It contains Hammurabi's legal code and is topped with an image of the king receiving the law from the sun god, **Shamash**.

Inscription (Excerpt from the Laws of Hammurabi):

"When Marduk sent me to rule over the people, to give protection to the land, I established law and justice in the language of the land, and I promoted the welfare of the people."

"If a man strikes the cheek of a superior, he shall receive sixty blows with an ox-hide whip in public."

"If a man puts out the eye of another man, his eye shall be put out."

"If a man breaks the bone of another man, his bone shall be broken."

"If a slave says to his master, 'You are not my master,' his ear shall be cut off."

2. The Victory Stele of Naram-Sin (Circa 2254–2218 BCE)

Context: This stele commemorates the victory of **Naram-Sin**, the Akkadian king, over the Lullubi people. It depicts Naram-Sin ascending a mountain, wearing a horned helmet symbolizing divinity, with his army following him.

Inscription (Partial Translation):

"Naram-Sin, mighty king of Akkad, favored by the gods, has conquered the rebellious Lullubi in the name of Enlil and Inanna. He, the exalted one, has ascended the mountains, and his enemies lie at his feet, crushed by the power of his divine favor."

"The people of Akkad are victorious. The king, Naram-Sin, is granted kingship by the gods, and his enemies are scattered like dust."

3. The Stele of Ur-Nammu (Circa 2100 BCE)

Context: This stele commemorates the deeds of **Ur-Nammu**, the founder of the Third Dynasty of Ur. It includes praises for the king's piety and his construction of temples, canals, and ziggurats.

Inscription (Partial Translation):

"I, Ur-Nammu, the mighty warrior, king of Ur, builder of temples for the gods, have restored the great ziggurat of

Nanna. By the grace of the gods, I have cleared the fields, dug canals, and brought prosperity to the people."

"The god Enlil has granted me strength and victory over my enemies. The lands are at peace, and the people prosper under my reign."

4. The Stele of Eannatum (Circa 2500 BCE) – Also known as the Stele of the Vultures

Context: This stele records the victory of **Eannatum**, ruler of Lagash, over the neighboring city-state of Umma. The relief depicts vultures carrying away the heads of the defeated enemies.

Inscription (Partial Translation):

"Eannatum, mighty ruler of Lagash, has been blessed by Ningirsu, the god of war. I have defeated the wicked forces of Umma, and their bodies lie scattered on the battlefield."

"By the power of Ningirsu, I have restored the boundary markers of Lagash and reclaimed the fields stolen by Umma."

"Let all who see this stele know: the might of Lagash and the gods shall protect this land, and no enemy shall stand against us."

5. The Stele of the Vultures (Lagash)

Context: This famous monument was erected to commemorate the military victory of the city-state of Lagash over Umma and is named for the vultures depicted in the relief, which symbolize the aftermath of battle.

Inscription (Partial Translation):

"For Ningirsu, the mighty warrior god, Eannatum, the ruler of Lagash, has conquered the city of Umma. The enemy is vanquished, and their fields are ours once more. Their bones lie broken upon the earth, and vultures feast upon their remains."

"This stele marks the boundary between Lagash and Umma. Let no man disturb it, for the wrath of Ningirsu shall come upon him."

---

6. Gudea's Statue Inscriptions (Circa 2144–2124 BCE)

Context: Gudea, ruler of Lagash, commissioned many statues of himself, often with inscriptions celebrating his construction of temples and devotion to the gods.

Inscription (Example from Statue B):

"I am Gudea, ruler of Lagash, shepherd of the people, beloved of Ningirsu. I have built the house of Ningirsu, the Eninnu temple, as an offering to my lord."

"In the year of my reign, I brought peace and prosperity to the land, and I offered abundant gifts to the gods. The people of Lagash are safe under my rule."

"May my name be remembered for all time, as the king who served the gods and his people with justice and wisdom."

---

7. The Stele of Manishtushu (Circa 2270 BCE)

Context: **Manishtushu**, an Akkadian king, had steles created to commemorate his victories and the expansion of his empire.

Inscription (Partial Translation):

"Manishtushu, king of Akkad, who has extended the boundaries of his land from the mountains to the sea. By the will of the gods, I have conquered Elam and brought its treasures back to Akkad."

"I have built temples to Enlil and Enki, and I have brought order and prosperity to the land. May my name be remembered for my victories and for the favor of the gods."

---

8. The Obelisk of Hammurabi

Context: Hammurabi, the Babylonian king, erected obelisks and steles to commemorate his legal reforms, military victories, and dedication to the gods.

Inscription (Partial Translation):

"I, Hammurabi, king of Babylon, the just ruler chosen by the gods, have restored peace and order to the land. I have established laws that are fair and just for the people, and I have defeated my enemies on the battlefield."

"May the gods Marduk and Shamash bless my reign, and may Babylon prosper under my rule."

9. The Black Obelisk of Shalmaneser III (Circa 858–824 BCE)

Context: The **Black Obelisk of Shalmaneser III** is one of the most significant Assyrian monuments. It commemorates the military campaigns of **Shalmaneser III**, king of Assyria, and includes a depiction of the tribute paid by King Jehu of Israel.

Inscription (Partial Translation):

"Shalmaneser, king of Assyria, conqueror of the lands from the rising to the setting of the sun. I have subjugated the kings of the earth, and they have brought their tribute before me."

"Jehu, son of Omri, has bowed before me and has brought silver, gold, and gifts as tribute. The might of Assyria is unchallenged, and all lands tremble at my name."

10. The Nabonidus Cylinder (Circa 556–539 BCE)

Context: The **Cylinders of Nabonidus**, created by the last king of the Neo-Babylonian Empire, contain inscriptions about the king's restoration of temples and his devotion to the god Sin.

Inscription (Partial Translation):

"I, Nabonidus, king of Babylon, have restored the temple of Sin in Harran. The gods have favored me, and I have rebuilt the temples of the great gods of Babylon."

"May the god Sin bless my reign, and may I continue to rule in peace and prosperity. I have restored the land, and the gods are pleased with my offerings."

Conclusion

These **Inscriptions on Monuments and Steles** are key historical sources that offer invaluable insight into the accomplishments, religious beliefs, and political ideologies of ancient Mesopotamian rulers. Carved into stone to endure through the ages, these inscriptions were not only declarations of power and divine favor but also served to legitimize the authority of kings by tying their reigns to the will of the gods. Each stele or monument inscription played a vital role in the propaganda of the time, ensuring that the deeds of the rulers were immortalized for posterity.

The Instructions of Shuruppak

is one of the oldest known literary texts from ancient Mesopotamia. Dating back to around 2600 BCE, this work is a set of proverbs and wisdom teachings attributed to **Shuruppak**, a king of the city of Shuruppak, and it provides guidance on how to live a moral, responsible, and prosperous life. The text is framed as advice from a father (King Shuruppak) to his son, **Ziusudra** (who is often identified as the hero of the Sumerian flood story, similar to Noah in the Bible).

The wisdom in the **Instructions of Shuruppak** covers a wide range of topics, including respect for the gods, proper behavior, justice, self-discipline, the importance of listening, and the consequences of wrongdoing. While the text is fragmentary, many of its proverbs and instructions have been reconstructed from various versions found on cuneiform tablets.

- **Found**: Tablets containing the *Instructions of Shuruppak* were found in various ancient Sumerian cities, including Abu Salabikh and Nippur.
- **Currently housed**:

  - Fragments of the *Instructions of Shuruppak* are housed in the **Iraq Museum**, Baghdad, and the **British Museum**, London.
  - Additional fragments are held in the **Penn Museum**, Philadelphia.

The Instructions of Shuruppak

Prologue:

O son of mine, Ziusudra, heed my words!
Let my instructions guide you, and let my wisdom strengthen you.
Listen to the advice of your father, for it shall protect you in the days to come.

Respect for the Gods and Elders

1. **Do not neglect the gods**, for their favor sustains the world. Make offerings to them in times of prosperity and need, and your path will be clear.
2. **Honor your mother and father**. Their wisdom has brought you into this world. Heed their counsel, for they have walked the path of life before you.
3. **Show respect to your elders**. Do not speak ill of them, and let their knowledge guide you. A wise man learns from those who have come before him.

On Speech and Silence

4. **Guard your tongue**. Do not speak harshly, for words have the power to destroy as well as to heal. A sharp tongue cuts deeper than any sword.
5. **Do not speak excessively**. Too much talk brings confusion, while silence often brings clarity. Know when to listen and when to speak.

6. **Do not tell lies**. Falsehoods will turn against you, and the truth, though it may be painful, will always prevail.
7. **Do not gossip**. Slander spreads like wildfire and will consume both the speaker and the listener. Instead, speak words that build up and encourage others.

On Justice and Integrity

8. **Do not take bribes**. Injustice destroys the foundation of society, and a man who accepts a bribe will be remembered with contempt.
9. **Treat all men fairly**. Whether rich or poor, noble or commoner, all are equal in the eyes of the gods. Show justice in your dealings.
10. **Do not exploit the weak**. The gods look favorably upon those who defend the powerless. Protect the orphan, the widow, and the stranger, for they have no one else to turn to.
11. **Judge justly**. When called upon to settle disputes, weigh all sides carefully. The judgment of a fair ruler brings peace, but injustice leads to chaos.

On Wisdom and Knowledge

12. **Seek wisdom in all things**. A wise man is one who listens, learns, and seeks understanding. Wisdom will be your shield in times of trouble.
13. **Do not stop learning**. Knowledge is a treasure that can never be taken from you. The man who seeks

knowledge will grow stronger with each passing day.
14. **Avoid foolishness**. Do not waste your time with idle talk and trivial pursuits. A wise man seeks to understand the world, while a fool chases after empty pleasures.

On Wealth and Prosperity

15. **Do not covet your neighbor's wealth**. What is his is his by the will of the gods, and envy will only bring you ruin. Work honestly for what you have.
16. **Be diligent in your work**. A lazy man invites poverty into his home, but the diligent man prospers. Work hard, and your fields will yield abundance.
17. **Do not hoard wealth**. Share what you have with others, for the gods bless the generous man. Wealth is fleeting, but the gratitude of others is lasting.

On Friendship and Loyalty

18. **Choose your friends wisely**. A good friend will stand by you in times of trouble, but a false friend will abandon you when you need him most.
19. **Be loyal to your companions**. A man's loyalty is his most prized possession. Stand by your friends, and they will stand by you.
20. **Do not betray trust**. Trust is hard to earn and easily lost. A man who betrays his friend will find himself alone in his time of need.

On Conduct and Behavior

21. **Do not seek quarrels**. A man who loves conflict will find himself surrounded by enemies. Be a peacemaker, and others will look to you for guidance.
22. **Control your temper**. Anger clouds the mind and leads to poor decisions. A calm and measured man is respected, while a hot-tempered man is feared and avoided.
23. **Do not steal**. The man who steals will always live in fear, for his crime will eventually be discovered. What is gained through theft is lost twice as quickly.
24. **Do not be greedy**. Greed leads a man to ruin, for he will never be satisfied. Be content with what the gods have given you, and you will know peace.

On Family and Marriage

25. **Cherish your wife**. A good wife is a gift from the gods, and she will bring joy and stability to your household. Treat her with respect and kindness.
26. **Teach your children well**. A father's wisdom shapes the future of his children. Guide them with love and discipline, and they will bring honor to your name.
27. **Protect your household**. A man's home is his sanctuary, and it is his duty to keep it safe. Defend your family, and the gods will defend you.

On Fate and the Gods

28. **Do not defy the will of the gods**. Their plans are beyond our understanding, and to fight against them is futile. Accept what they have decreed, and live in harmony with their will.
29. **Do not question the workings of fate**. Some things are not meant for man to know. Trust in the wisdom of the gods, for they see what we cannot.
30. **Offer sacrifices and prayers**. The gods bless those who honor them with offerings and devotion. Seek their favor, and they will guide your steps.

Epilogue:

My son, Ziusudra, may these instructions be written upon your heart. May they guide you through the trials of life, protect you from harm, and bring you wisdom and prosperity.
Remember your father's words, and pass them on to your sons, so that they too may walk the path of righteousness.

Conclusion

The **Instructions of Shuruppak** represent one of the earliest forms of didactic literature, imparting moral and practical wisdom for living a righteous life in harmony with society and the gods. These proverbs and teachings offer timeless lessons on the importance of justice, self-control, respect, hard work, and humility.

The text not only reflects the moral values of ancient Sumer but also serves as a foundation for later wisdom literature, including biblical texts such as Proverbs and Ecclesiastes. Its focus on family, community, and religious devotion provides insight into the Sumerians' worldview and their emphasis on living in accordance with divine will.

Cylinder seals

are small, carved cylindrical objects used in ancient Mesopotamia to create impressions on clay. These seals were rolled over wet clay to leave a continuous design, serving both practical and symbolic purposes. They were commonly used as a form of personal identification, much like a signature, for securing documents, marking property, and authorizing transactions. The inscriptions and images on cylinder seals often depicted gods, mythical creatures, or daily life and were intricately carved with great skill.

Because cylinder seals were individualized objects, they don't contain long, continuous texts like tablets or steles. Instead, each seal typically features a unique combination of symbols, inscriptions (if any), and images that convey ownership or authority. Many cylinder seals feature inscriptions that include:

- The name of the owner.
- Titles or professions (e.g., priest, king, scribe).
- References to deities or divine favor.

Below is a representation of what typical **cylinder seal inscriptions** might include, along with descriptions of the images that might accompany the text.

- **Found**: Cylinder seals have been found in many Sumerian sites, including Ur, Uruk, Lagash, and Nippur. They were often discovered in temples, tombs, or alongside other administrative documents.
- **Currently housed**:
    - Many Sumerian cylinder seals are held in the **British Museum**, London.

- **Metropolitan Museum of Art**, New York.
- **Louvre Museum**, Paris.
- **Iraq Museum**, Baghdad.

Cylinder Seal of a Sumerian Priest

Inscriptions (as found on the seal):

"I, Enki-nasir, devoted servant of Enlil, priest of the temple of Nippur, seek the blessings of the gods."

Description of Imagery:
The seal depicts Enki-nasir standing before the god **Enlil**, who is seated on a throne. Enlil holds a scepter, symbolizing his divine authority, while the priest raises his hands in prayer. Behind the priest are symbols of the crescent moon and the stars, indicating divine presence and cosmic order. Beneath the scene is a depiction of the sacred ziggurat of Nippur, the temple of Enlil.

Cylinder Seal of a Merchant

Inscriptions (as found on the seal):

"Lugal-Eresh, merchant of Lagash, under the protection of Ningirsu, brings goods from Dilmun."

Description of Imagery:
This seal shows a boat sailing across the sea, symbolizing trade and long-distance commerce. Lugal-Eresh, the

merchant, is depicted leading donkeys laden with goods, such as jars of oil and sacks of grain. The god **Ningirsu** stands above the scene, holding a lightning bolt, signifying his protection over the merchant's travels. Fish and waves are engraved beneath the boat to represent the journey over water.

Cylinder Seal of a Sumerian King

Inscriptions (as found on the seal):

"Ur-Nammu, king of Ur, favored of Nanna, builder of temples and protector of the people."

Description of Imagery:
The seal depicts **Ur-Nammu** standing before the moon god **Nanna**, who sits upon a throne with a crescent moon symbol above him. Ur-Nammu holds a building tool, representing his role as the builder of temples. Soldiers stand behind the king, indicating his authority as a protector of the realm. At the base of the scene, artisans are shown constructing a ziggurat.

Cylinder Seal of a Scribe

Inscriptions (as found on the seal):

"Dudu, scribe of Uruk, servant of Inanna, who records the deeds of kings."

Description of Imagery:
The seal shows **Dudu** seated with a stylus in hand,

inscribing a tablet. The goddess **Inanna** stands beside him, holding a bow and arrows, symbolizing her role as a warrior goddess. In the background are the walls of the city of Uruk, signifying the scribe's connection to the royal court and the city's governance. The writing tools (stylus, clay tablet) are prominently depicted to highlight the scribe's profession.

Cylinder Seal of a High Priestess

Inscriptions (as found on the seal):

"Enheduanna, high priestess of Nanna, daughter of Sargon, blessed by the moon god."

Description of Imagery:
The seal portrays **Enheduanna** in a ceremonial robe, standing before the temple of Nanna. The moon god **Nanna** is shown seated on a throne, offering his blessing to Enheduanna, who raises her hands in reverence. Behind her, attendants carry offerings of bread, wine, and incense. The scene includes celestial symbols—stars, the moon, and the sun—reflecting her divine connection to Nanna.

Cylinder Seal of a Craftsman

Inscriptions (as found on the seal):

"Anzu, master craftsman of Ur, who shapes the treasures of the gods."

Description of Imagery:
The seal illustrates **Anzu** working at a forge, hammering a piece of metal into shape. Tools such as hammers, chisels, and tongs are prominently displayed. Above the craftsman is the god **Enki**, the god of wisdom and crafts, who blesses the workshop with streams of water (representing creativity and life). Figures of lions and bulls, symbolizing strength and craftsmanship, are shown alongside the craftsman's work.

Cylinder Seal of a Military Commander

Inscriptions (as found on the seal):

"Lugal-anda, commander of the armies of Lagash, favored by Ningirsu, the warrior god."

Description of Imagery:
The seal shows **Lugal-anda** leading soldiers into battle, with chariots and spears prominently displayed. The god **Ningirsu** stands atop a mountain, holding a weapon, blessing the army's efforts. Soldiers are depicted carrying shields and swords, advancing toward a fortified city. The inscription indicates the divine favor that the commander seeks before entering battle.

Description of Cylinder Seal Use and Significance

Cylinder seals were not just practical tools; they were deeply symbolic. Each individual or official would carry a seal that represented their authority, role, or divine favor. These seals were used to authenticate documents, seal goods for trade, or mark property as belonging to a certain person or temple. They were often rolled over the wet clay of a contract, tablet, or door to create a permanent mark of ownership or legitimacy. The imagery on each seal was carefully chosen to represent the owner's social or professional role, their relationship with a deity, or their achievements.

Because cylinder seals were often personalized, they provide rich information about the people who used them and the society they lived in. Their artistry also reflects the skills of ancient craftsmen, who intricately carved these small cylinders with remarkable precision.

Conclusion

The **cylinder seals** from ancient Mesopotamia were personal, symbolic objects that conveyed authority, identity, and divine favor. While they do not contain long, narrative texts, the inscriptions on these seals—combined with the images carved into them—offer a wealth of information about the roles, professions, and beliefs of their owners. These small, portable artifacts served a vital role in the bureaucratic and daily life of ancient Sumerians, making them some of the most significant pieces of ancient writing and art.

Enheduanna,

daughter of the Akkadian king Sargon of Akkad (circa 2285–2250 BCE), is considered one of the earliest known authors in history. As a high priestess of the moon god **Nanna** in the city of Ur, she composed a series of hymns that have survived in various forms, including those dedicated to the goddess **Inanna** (Ishtar), as well as other temples and deities in the Sumerian pantheon. These hymns reflect her deep religious devotion, her political influence as a priestess, and her poetic mastery.

Her most famous work is the **Exaltation of Inanna**, but she also composed the **Temple Hymns**, which were dedicated to various gods and their sacred sites. Below is a reconstruction of some of her most important hymns.

The Exaltation of Inanna (Nin-Me-Sar-Ra)

This hymn, also known as *"Lady of My Heart,"* is Enheduanna's most famous and is dedicated to the goddess Inanna. It celebrates Inanna's power, beauty, and might, while also reflecting Enheduanna's personal devotion and struggles.

- **Found**: These hymns were found primarily in the city of Ur (modern-day Tell el-Muqayyar, Iraq) in temple archives.
- **Currently housed**:

  - The hymns and other related tablets are located in the **Penn Museum**, Philadelphia, and the **British Museum**, London.
  - Other fragments are in the **Iraq Museum**, Baghdad.

Lines 1–10:

Lady of all the divine powers,
Radiant light, righteous woman clothed in radiance,
Beloved of An and Uraš,
Mistress of heaven,
With the great diadem, you wear the heavens as your crown!
The stars are your jewels,
You are the high priestess of the highest heaven,
The fate of all lands rests in your hands.
At your command, they bow before you.
Heaven and earth tremble at your word!

Lines 11–20:

Great light of all lands, crowned with the heavens,
At your command, life flourishes,
At your command, destruction falls.
O righteous lady, none dare challenge your might!
In the pure heavens, your word is the final word,
And no god or mortal may defy your command.
The world bows before you, queen of battle and love,
Mistress of all the great powers.
The fate of all the peoples lies in your hands.
The mountains kneel, the rivers bow to your might.

Lines 21–30:

O powerful Inanna, you who ride upon the storm,
Your voice echoes across the lands, shaking the earth,
The heavens tremble at your roar!
Your fury brings destruction to the wicked,
And your mercy grants life to the righteous.
The earth and sky are yours, your reign is eternal.
You alone bring the flood, you alone bring life.
Before you, all gods stand in awe,
For your might surpasses all others.
Your name is great across the lands.

Lines 31–40:

Mistress of battle, you guide the armies,
Victorious in all wars, you wield the sword of heaven!
At your command, the shields are raised,
At your call, the spears fly.
O fierce lady, you bring ruin to those who defy you,
And you lift up the heads of the humble.
In your hand lies victory,
You are the shining flame that burns the wicked,
The light of life for those who follow you.
Your power knows no equal!

Lines 41–50:

I, Enheduanna, your servant,
I have offered you praise, O radiant one.
I have seen the power of your hand,
I have witnessed your wrath and your mercy.

Before you, I have lifted my hands in devotion,
And my heart has sought your guidance.
May my song of praise reach your ears,
May you look upon me with favor.
For I, Enheduanna, am yours, O Inanna,
And I offer you my heart, my words, my life.

The Temple Hymns

Enheduanna also composed a series of hymns dedicated to various temples throughout Sumer. These hymns celebrate the gods and goddesses who inhabit these temples and emphasize the importance of the temple as a sacred space, connecting heaven and earth. Below are some selected examples.

Hymn 1: The Temple of Enlil in Nippur

O E-kur, house of the great mountain,

Sanctuary of Enlil, father of all gods,

Your walls are vast, reaching to the heavens,

Your gates stand strong, welcoming the faithful.

Within your halls, the fate of all lands is decreed.

O Enlil, lord of the storm,

In your temple, the light of truth shines brightly.

The mountains bow before you, the rivers flow at your command.

Hymn 2: The Temple of Nanna in Ur

O E-gishnugal, radiant house of the moon god,

Home of Nanna, who illuminates the night.

Your brilliance spreads across the heavens,

And the people look to you for guidance.

O Nanna, lord of the night sky,

Your light is eternal, and your temple is blessed.

In your sacred chamber, the prayers of the people rise like incense.

Hymn 3: The Temple of Inanna in Uruk

O Eanna, great house of Inanna,

Mistress of heaven and earth,

Your splendor is unmatched, your beauty is eternal.

O Inanna, lady of love and war,

Your temple is the heart of Uruk,

And in your sanctuary, the people offer their hearts.

Hymn 4: The Temple of Ningirsu in Lagash

O E-ninnu, house of the mighty Ningirsu,

The warrior god who defends the city.

Your walls are strong, your gates are unshakable.

O Ningirsu, protector of Lagash,

Your temple is a fortress of strength,

And your people find peace within your walls.

Hymn 5: The Temple of Ninhursag in Adab

O E-kur, house of the earth mother Ninhursag,

The source of all life, the nurturer of all lands.

O Ninhursag, lady of fertility and growth,

Your temple is a garden of abundance,

And in your presence, the earth blooms with life.

Hymn 6: The Temple of Utu in Sippar

O E-babbar, house of the shining Utu,

Lord of the sun, who brings light to the world.

Your temple is a beacon of justice,

And in your halls, the truth is revealed.

O Utu, the just and righteous one,

Your light shines upon all lands,

And your people find guidance in your wisdom.

Hymn 7: The Temple of Ninurta in Nippur

O E-meslam, house of Ninurta,

The warrior god who crushes the wicked.

Your temple is a fortress of might,

And your enemies tremble at your approach.

O Ninurta, lord of victory,

In your temple, the banners of triumph are raised,

And your people are victorious under your command.

Conclusion

Enheduanna's hymns are some of the earliest recorded examples of religious devotion, celebrating the might, power, and majesty of the gods while emphasizing the role of the priestess in maintaining the sacred order. Her works reflect the complexity of Sumerian religion, where gods were intimately connected with the cities they protected and the temples where they were worshipped.

Through her hymns, Enheduanna not only expressed her personal faith and devotion but also reinforced the political and religious authority of her family, especially her father, King Sargon, and his Akkadian empire. As a high priestess, she served as an intermediary between the gods and the people, and her poetry played a central role in legitimizing the divine favor bestowed upon her lineage.

Summary of Key Museums and Locations:

- **Iraq Museum** (Baghdad, Iraq): Houses a large number of Sumerian artifacts, including tablets, inscriptions, and seals.
- **British Museum** (London, UK): Holds important artifacts like fragments of the *Epic of Gilgamesh*, administrative texts, and cylinder seals.
- **Louvre Museum** (Paris, France): Home to significant pieces like the *Stele of the Vultures* and religious inscriptions.

- **Penn Museum** (Philadelphia, USA): Contains a wide range of Sumerian texts, including fragments of the *Code of Ur-Nammu* and economic tablets.
- **Ashmolean Museum** (Oxford, UK): Houses a notable copy of the *Sumerian King List*.
- **Istanbul Archaeological Museums** (Turkey): Contains fragments of Sumerian laws and economic records.

These texts and artifacts offer rich insights into the life, laws, religion, and politics of the Sumerians, and their current preservation in various museums allows researchers to continue studying this early civilization.

Conclusion

This collection of **Sumerian hymns, prayers, inscriptions, and ancient texts** reflects the profound connection between the people of ancient Mesopotamia and their gods, rulers, and societal structures. The works of **Enheduanna**, the wisdom of **Shuruppak**, the legal and administrative records of ancient kings, and the deeply symbolic use of cylinder seals all offer invaluable insights into a world where the divine and the earthly were intertwined in every aspect of life.

From the earliest laws to poetic praises of deities, these texts illustrate the Sumerians' sense of order, justice, and reverence for the forces that governed their universe. The kings and priests saw themselves as mediators between the divine and the mortal, with their actions affecting the fate of their people, cities, and lands. As seen in the **Temple Hymns**, the gods were not distant figures; they were active participants in the daily lives of the people, with their favor sought through ritual, devotion, and offerings.

Enheduanna's hymns, particularly her **Exaltation of Inanna**, reveal the powerful role of women in the religious life of Sumer, as well as the intricate relationship between political power and religious authority. Her words have transcended millennia, making her not only a historical figure of her time but a voice that continues to resonate today.

The **Sumerian King List**, **Code of Ur-Nammu**, and other administrative and economic tablets highlight the importance of law, order, and governance in the flourishing city-states of Sumer. These texts demonstrate the Sumerians' concern for justice, fairness, and the efficient management of resources, as well as their understanding of legacy and the preservation of power.

Finally, the inscriptions on **monuments and steles** serve as eternal reminders of the accomplishments and aspirations of Sumerian rulers, whose reigns were legitimized by the favor of the gods. These inscriptions allowed them to carve their names into history, ensuring that their deeds would be remembered for all time.

In conclusion, the writings of ancient Sumer offer us a window into one of the earliest civilizations known to humanity. They reveal the values, beliefs, and systems that shaped their society, showing us that even thousands of years ago, humans grappled with the same questions of morality, justice, faith, and legacy that we do today. The endurance of these texts stands as a testament to the Sumerians' remarkable contributions to human culture, knowledge, and spirituality, leaving an indelible mark on the development of civilization.

Appendices

Appendix A: Timeline of Sumerian Civilization

Date (BCE)	Event
c. 4500–4000	Ubaid Period: Earliest settlement of Sumerian cities.
c. 3500–2900	Uruk Period: Development of city-states, early writing.
c. 2900–2334	Early Dynastic Period: Formation of Sumerian city-states (Ur, Uruk, Lagash, etc.).
c. 2600	The Instructions of Shuruppak composed.
c. 2334–2279	Reign of Sargon of Akkad, beginning of the Akkadian Empire.
c. 2285–2250	Enheduanna, daughter of Sargon, serves as high priestess and composes hymns.
c. 2112–2004	Third Dynasty of Ur: Period of prosperity and cultural flourishing, **Code of Ur-Nammu** written.
c. 1900–1600	Old Babylonian Period: Hammurabi rules, **Code of Hammurabi** inscribed.
539	Fall of Babylon to the Persian Empire.

Appendix B: Glossary of Key Terms

- **Cuneiform**: The wedge-shaped writing system developed by the Sumerians, used for recording laws, literature, administrative records, and other texts.
- **Cylinder Seals**: Small, cylindrical objects engraved with designs and inscriptions, used to create

impressions on wet clay to authenticate documents or mark property.
- **Enheduanna**: The high priestess of the moon god Nanna in Ur, daughter of King Sargon of Akkad, and the first known author in history.
- **E-kur**: The temple dedicated to Enlil, the chief god of Sumer, located in Nippur.
- **Inanna**: Sumerian goddess of love, fertility, and warfare, often associated with the planet Venus. She was one of the most prominent deities in the Sumerian pantheon.
- **Lugal**: Sumerian term for "king" or "ruler."
- **Nanna**: The Sumerian moon god, worshipped primarily in the city of Ur.
- **Stele**: A stone or wooden slab, often inscribed or carved, used as a monument or marker to commemorate significant events or proclaim laws.
- **Ziggurat**: A large, stepped structure that served as the center of worship in Sumerian cities, dedicated to the city's patron deity.

Appendix C: List of Sumerian Deities

Deity	Role/Description
An/Anu	The sky god and supreme ruler of the heavens in Sumerian mythology.
Enlil	God of air, wind, and storms, considered the king of the gods and ruler of the earth.
Enki/Ea	God of water, wisdom, and creation, known for his intelligence and generosity.
Inanna/Ishtar	Goddess of love, fertility, and war; also associated with the planet Venus.
Nanna/Sin	God of the moon, worshipped in Ur. Father

Deity	Role/Description
	of Inanna and Utu.
Ningirsu	Warrior god and patron deity of the city-state of Lagash.
Ninhursag	Earth goddess, associated with fertility and the mountains.
Utu/Shamash	God of the sun and justice, protector of truth and fairness.
Ninurta	God of war and hunting, protector of the fields.

Appendix D: The Writing System – Cuneiform

Cuneiform is the earliest known writing system developed by the Sumerians around 3400–3000 BCE. Originally used for recording economic transactions, cuneiform evolved into a more complex system for writing literature, laws, and religious texts.

- **Development**: Cuneiform began as pictographs, with simple drawings representing objects or concepts. Over time, these pictographs became more abstract and stylized, eventually becoming wedge-shaped marks that could be quickly inscribed on clay tablets using a reed stylus.
- **Types of Texts**: Cuneiform was used to record a wide variety of documents, including:
    - **Administrative tablets**: Lists of goods, taxes, and resources.
    - **Legal codes**: Laws, such as the Code of Ur-Nammu and the Code of Hammurabi.
    - **Literature**: Epic poetry, hymns, and wisdom literature (e.g., the *Epic of Gilgamesh*).

- ○ **Religious texts**: Prayers, temple hymns, and rituals.
- **Languages**: Though initially developed by the Sumerians, cuneiform was later adapted for use in other languages, including Akkadian, Babylonian, and Assyrian.

Appendix E: Sample Translations from the Code of Ur-Nammu

The **Code of Ur-Nammu** (circa 2100–2050 BCE) is one of the oldest known law codes. Here are examples of surviving laws from the code:

1. **If a man commits murder, that man must be killed.**
2. **If a man commits robbery, he is to be killed.**
3. **If a man commits kidnapping, he is to be imprisoned and pay 15 shekels of silver.**
4. **If a man causes the loss of another man's eye, he must pay half a mina of silver.**
5. **If a man breaks another man's bone, he must pay one mina of silver.**

Appendix F: The Role of Enheduanna

Enheduanna, as the high priestess of Nanna, played a crucial role in consolidating her father's empire through her religious and literary contributions. As one of the first known authors in human history, her works are foundational to Sumerian literature and offer insight into the political and religious life of ancient Mesopotamia. Her hymns to Inanna reflect her devotion, struggles, and influence, marking her as a powerful spiritual and political figure.

Appendix G: Famous Sumerian Monuments and Steles

- **Stele of Hammurabi**: A stone slab inscribed with the Code of Hammurabi, one of the earliest and most complete legal codes.
- **Victory Stele of Naram-Sin**: Commemorates the Akkadian king's victory over the Lullubi people, depicting Naram-Sin as a godlike figure.
- **Stele of the Vultures**: A monument erected by the ruler Eannatum of Lagash to celebrate his victory over Umma, featuring dramatic depictions of battle.
- **Nabonidus Cylinders**: Inscriptions by the Neo-Babylonian king Nabonidus detailing his restoration of temples and devotion to the god Sin.

Appendix H: Major Sumerian Cities and Their Temples

City	Deity	Temple
Ur	Nanna (Moon God)	E-gishnugal (House of the Great Light)
Uruk	Inanna (Love, War)	Eanna (House of Heaven)
Nippur	Enlil (Storm God)	E-kur (Mountain House)
Lagash	Ningirsu (War	E-ninnu (House of the Warrior)

City	Deity	Temple
Eridu	Enki (Water God)	Abzu (House of the Abyss)

Appendix I: Legacy of Sumerian Literature and Culture

Sumerian literature and religious texts have had a lasting impact on subsequent cultures and civilizations. Many of the themes found in Sumerian myths, such as the concept of divine kingship, the struggle between order and chaos, and the search for immortality, are echoed in later Mesopotamian literature, the Hebrew Bible, and Greek mythology.

Sumerians were pioneers in literature, law, and city-building, laying the foundation for many aspects of modern civilization. Their innovations in writing, governance, and religion continue to influence contemporary studies of history, archaeology, and ancient languages.

This collection of appendices offers further context and understanding of the intricate and diverse writings of Sumerian civilization, from legal codes and hymns to temple rituals and administrative records. Together, they provide a comprehensive look at the earliest recorded history of human society.